4TH SECTOR ENTREPRENEURSHIP

Grow sustainable social impact without losing your mind

BEN FREEDMAN & CRAIG CAREY

WRITING MATTERS

The 4th Sector Entrepreneurship

Ben Freedman and Craig Carey

First published in November 2019

Writing Matters Publishing (UK)

ISBN 978-1-912774-43-2 (Pbk)
ISBN 978-1-912774-42-5 (Kindle)

A CIP catalogue record for this book is available from the British Library.

Contents

Acknowledgments

The ideas put forward in these pages are built on the thoughts and work of many people.

We're especially indebted to Jubilee Barrow, Andrew Priestley, Andrew Bailey, Eddy Canfor-Dumas, Andrew Croft, Patrick Donovan, Michelle Livingston, Deri Llewellyn-Davies, Alistair Lobo, Peter Osborn, Carrie Ward, our current and past clients and our interviewees; all of whom have significantly helped shape our thinking over many years.

We're also hugely grateful to friends and colleagues who took the time and trouble to read the text in its various drafts and offered many helpful challenges, criticisms and suggestions.

And finally, thank you to Sue and Anna and our children for putting up with us; and your ongoing encouragement.

Introduction

'In a world deluged by irrelevant information, clarity is power.'

Yuval Harari, *21 Lessons for the 21st Century*

When it was suggested that we should write a book our coach Andrew Priestley gave us some very simple advice: Decide what you want to say, write for one hour every day but above all be very clear who you're speaking to.

So, who do you think we are?

In the fifty years that we have between us spent in running organisations and trying to create social impact, we have come to realise that we don't really fit into any of what would be considered by many to be the three key sectors of the economy – private, public and not-for-profit.

The business world is too focused on simply keeping score through money, government is too hierarchical and not-for-profit too stifling.

We feel we belong in a *4th Sector* where the enterprise of business mixes with the sense of service of government and the compassion of not-for-profit to create a fertile ground for innovation and the creation of lasting social value.

Over time we have each become adept at recognising fellow travellers, mentally ticking off a checklist of attitudes and beliefs that make us all misfits from so much of traditional thinking, almost like members of a secret club.

People who have a clear sense of right despite the fact that everyone tells them that they're wrong.

People who don't like being told what to do.

People who are convinced there is a better way.

This book is written for you.

Clarity of Leadership, Strategy and Culture

Without exception, every *4th Sector* leader is driven to make a sustainable difference to some key area of social deficit. However, again without exception, they experience a level of frustration at not being able to do enough.

So what gets in the way?

What we have understood as we have listened over the years is that almost every barrier can be grouped under one of three headings:

- **Confused Leadership** - a lack of clarity around *purpose, vision and values* (both personally and organisationally), their customers and how they're positioned in the market by the unique solutions they offer.
- **Confused Strategy** – a lack of clarity of how to plan to maximise value out of the key areas of strategy – marketing, sales, finance, operations, social impact, digital and talent.
- **Confused Culture** – a lack of a clear enterprise mindset and behaviour within their organisation that's so essential to *get sh*t done.*

If you recognise yourself in any part of this we have structured this book in a way to help you address this confusion.

Key Parts Of The Book

The book is broken down into six parts.

Part 1 considers the world of the *4th Sector*, why it's needed and the difficulties it creates for you as leaders in having to serve multiple masters. So, why would anyone choose to become a *4th Sector Entrepreneur*? We also offer some answers to that question.

Part 2 suggests some ways in which you can lay a solid foundation that allows you to work on your enterprise rather than in it.

Part 3 looks at how *Clarity of Leadership* is built on three principles:

1. A leader's clear personal *purpose, vision and values*, which are congruent with
2. The clear *purpose, vision and values* of their organisation and which are then fulfilled through
3. Clarity about what value you're providing for which customer's needs.

We then introduce a tool called *Strategy on a Page (SOAP)* which is highly effective first in helping you communicate this clarity to everyone involved with your organisation, internal and external; and then in helping you delegate responsibility for planning and execution throughout your organisation.

Part 4 covers *Clarity of Strategy,* giving an overview of the key areas you need to consider but then introducing our fourth principle, which is that Talent – hiring, developing and retaining the right people – is the most important strategy of them all.

Part 5, *Clarity of Culture,* looks at our final three principles – *Clarity of Measurement, Clarity of Execution* and *Clarity of Communication* - which together form the backbone of your organisational culture.

Finally, Part 6 introduces some meeting structures that bring everything together in a highly practical, day-to-day way.

Throughout the text we have also suggested a selection of simple exercises that you can do as you read – or you can come back to once you've finished reading the whole book.

Most of the exercises at the beginning of the chapters are intended to encourage you to consider the current reality of your enterprise today; while we hope those at the end offer valuable and practical application to drive action.

We look forward to hearing what you think.

Ben and Craig

Part 1
The 4th Sector

Chapter 1
Why A 4th Sector?

'We're doomed.'

Corporal Fraser, *Dad's Army*

One of the few things that people can agree on at a time of so much fractious debate is that our society faces numerous major challenges. Climate change, health and social care, education, public welfare, housing, the criminal justice system and the world of work in general all seem to be under constant threat. It's difficult at times not to hear the voice of Corporal Fraser from the much-loved sitcom, *Dad's Army.*

In the continuous search for innovative solutions everyone has their favourite approach.

Private Sector

For many, the key is business existing in a free and unregulated market, where individuals left to their own devices – i.e. once government gets out of the way – will naturally find the best answers.

Harvard Business School professor Michael Porter argues that *'businesses acting as business - not as charitable donors - are the most powerful force for addressing the pressing issues we face.'*[1]

As David Cameron asserted in 2011, 'Most public services could be run by private firms, charities and voluntary groups ... Public services should be open to a range of providers competing to offer a better service ... Instead of justifying why it makes sense to introduce competition in some public services ... the state will have to justify why it should ever operate a monopoly.'[2]

Indeed, in a 2018 public letter[3], described by the *Financial Times* as '*one of the most catalytic texts for the new era of purposeful capitalism*', Larry Fink, Chairman & CEO of *BlackRock,* one of the world's largest asset management firms, wrote that *'with governments failing to prepare for the future, people were looking to commercial companies to deliver not only financial performance but also a positive contribution to society, benefitting customers and communities, not just shareholders.'* Without social purpose, Fink contended, *'companies fail to make the investment in employees, innovation and capital expenditures needed for long term growth.'*

Yet, despite Fink's encouragement, too much of the business market remains driven by a desire for short-term gains for a very small number of its stakeholders.

As Andy Haldane, Chief Economist of the *Bank of England,* has noted, *'A majority of people do not trust business right now. One reason is a sense of fairness. For instance, if you look at the ratio of CEO pay to the pay of the average worker, in 1970 this ratio was around 20:1, whereas today in the US it's nearer 300:1.'*[4] And even the pro-business *Spectator* at times admits the private sector's shortcomings; for example, that '*Water firms promised efficiency. Instead they brought unsustainable debt. To use the words of the usually sedate Financial Times, they are an organised rip- off.'*[5]

Nor is business always the great innovator it's cracked up to be. For example, according to Professor Gill Kirton and Dr Cécile Guillaume, *'The privatisation of probation, carried out in the face of massive opposition from criminal justice experts, senior probation leaders... and the workers themselves, is unprecedented in terms of its scale and scope and has proven to be something of an unmitigated disaster for professionals.'*[6] The *FT* agrees. 'When the former Justice Secretary Chris Grayling decided to part-privatise the probation system six years ago he promised to inject *innovation and dynamism* into a struggling sector. The collapse of *Working Links*, a key provider, revealed the very opposite: a company crumbling under the financial strain of three loss-making contracts, managing ex-offenders so poorly that public safety was at risk.'[7]

Public Sector

Others argue that at such a time of crisis, only government has the resources and value system to be trusted to make the key decisions needed. According to the Labour Party's John McDonnell, for example, "Building an economy for the many also means bringing ownership and control of the utilities and key services into the hands of people who use and work in them. Rail, water, energy, Royal Mail: we're taking them back."[8]

The economists Mariana Mazzucato and William H Janeway[9] both argue eloquently that the state plays a fundamental role in real innovation in a way that so-called *venture capital* can't even consider. In recent times, for example, both the UK government's *Behavioural Insights Team (BIT)* - nicknamed the *nudge unit* - and its *Government Digital Service*, with the award-winning GOV.UK, have shown the power of government's ability to bring together enterprising individuals and give them free reign to innovate.[10]

Yet government ownership is far from ideal, as innovation and creativity are consistently suffocated by the rigidness of a top-down approach and influenced by short-term election cycles, political feuding and nervousness about media criticism.

Martin Wolf of the *FT* has summed up the case against public ownership. 'Contrary to Mr McDonnell's rhetorical flourish, nationalised industries were most definitely not in the hands of the people who used them. They were in the hands of ministers and civil servants who controlled them and the people who staffed them. They were chronically overmanned and heavily politicised. They either under-invested or made poor investment decisions. Not least, they treated users with indifference. This form of ownership didn't wither because it worked. It withered because it did not. That said, theory and experience demonstrate that privatisation is no panacea.'[11]

And too often government innovation ends badly. As a recent article on public sector IT disasters observes, *Time and again, when the public hears of a grandiose new IT scheme from government, it's matched by well-deserved scepticism from the old hands that have seen it all before.*[12]

To give just one example, a *2018 Public Accounts Committee* report on the IT modernisation of the Disclosure and Barring Service described it as *a masterclass in incompetency... Another example of a Home Office project marred by poor planning and contracting, delays, spiralling costs and a failure to understand what service users want.*[13]

Not-For-Profit Sector
Charity And Voluntary Sector Solutions

Finally, many people still focus on the role of *Not-For-Profits* to fill the gaps left by the limitations of both the market and the state.

The power of the charity sector is based on the recognition that giving to those in need seems to be a fundamental part of the human condition. As the *Charities Aid Foundation (CAF)* says, *'Charity makes you feel good'* and a lot of people in the UK seem to agree. They gave some £10.3bn to charities in 2017, while the *Charities Commission* at the beginning of 2018 listed more than 168,000 charities on its register, with a collective income from all sources of over £75bn – a record amount.

In the USA the sums are even greater. Bill Gates, Warren Buffet and others launched the *Giving Pledge* in 2010 to encourage billionaires to donate at least half of their wealth to charitable causes, during their lifetime or in their wills. A 2018 report from financial research company *Wealth-X* predicts the pledge may be worth as much as $600 billion by 2022.

Too often, however, the not-for-profit sector fails to drive innovation. There tends to be a fraught relationship with risk, arising from a lack of confidence in a consistency of income and a concern about respecting the trust placed in it by its donors. This in turn is compounded by underinvestment in talent development, coupled with rigidity within often bureaucratic governance structures managed by under-qualified trustees.

The net result is that good leadership and ideas can be stifled, while at times disaster can strike when decisions are taken without a robust risk-management process.

A prime example can be seen in the collapse in 2015 of *Kids Company,* an innovative organisation that ultimately imploded under the weight of its inadequate governance and underdeveloped management.

A 4th Sector....

So, three sectors of our economy are fighting their corner. All offer something of merit, yet with something in their DNA that inhibits the critical mass and quality of innovation that's essential to create the solutions so desperately needed in the gaps these sectors don't serve.

Meanwhile, sharing attributes of each of its bigger three siblings and sitting slightly outside the debate with its nose pressed against the window, is a fourth sector. Called variously the *Social Enterprise, Social Business, Profit with Purpose, Beyond Profit* or *Impact-Led Business* sector, it offers a vital and vibrant additional ingredient to the debate.

What Is A 4th Sector Organisation?

The idea of an enterprise driven by more than simple financial profit has been talked about increasingly in recent times – but what does it actually mean? What makes the sector unique? For *Social Enterprise UK (SEUK)*, the leading membership body for social enterprises in the UK, they're organisations that:[14]

- have a clear social and/or environmental mission set out in their governing documents
- generate the majority of their income through trade
- reinvest the majority of their profits
- are autonomous of the state
- are majority-controlled in the interests of their social mission
- are accountable and transparent

To qualify for the *Social Enterprise Mark* from the international accreditation authority, a social enterprise needs to meet the following criteria:[15]

- Be primarily dedicated to social objectives
- Be an independent business
- Be planning to become sustainable through trading income
- Be committed to dedicating a majority of any annual profit to social purposes
- Have an asset lock clause or similar
- Have a vision of how social objectives will be achieved

The *B Corp,* who offer a worldwide transparent best practice certification process, takes a wider view to include:

A new kind of business that balances purpose and profit ...

legally required to consider the impact of their decisions on their workers, customers, suppliers, community and the environment.[16]

It's our view, however, that a *4th Sector* organisation is as much about attitude and intent as a legal definition.

SEUK's 2018 report, *The Hidden Revolution,* states that *while any business can make claims about values, in a social enterprise those commitments are cultural and structural. Social Enterprises have to reinvest profits and have to put their social purpose above the pursuit of short-term financial gain... We are businesses that can be relied upon. To pursue always sustainable and inclusive growth... stay connected to our communities, pay our taxes and consider value over the wider longer-term.*[17]

Karen Lynch, Chief Executive of *BELU Water* in her interview for this book, sums it up well. "What I love about social enterprise is the joining together of people around positive intent. Every problem can be an opportunity. Rather than telling people they are bad, we align people around the good that can happen."

Yes, That's Nice, But...

What about all the stakeholders involved – customers, suppliers, staff, regulators, funders (often) and end-users? It really isn't possible to achieve a lot when running an organisation if you have to keep so many stakeholders happy, is it?

Well, the reality is that, in fact, it is.

Nationwide Building Society is the largest building society in the world and the world's seventh largest co-operative financial institution, with over 15 million members. *The Co-operative Group* is the largest consumer co-operative in the UK, with more than 4.5m active members and over 70,000 employees in some 4,200 locations.

In our opinion, both are *4th Sector* organisations.

As *The Hidden Revolution* notes: *'The social enterprise sector is worth £60bn to the UK economy and employs two million people. This represents 3% of GDP, three times the size of the agricultural industry and 5% of employment - as many jobs as the creative sector… Britain's top five co-operatives pay more tax than Amazon, Facebook, Apple, EBay and Starbucks combined.'*[18]

In addition, SEUK's analysis of the sector's impact on *NHS England* states that *'Social enterprises in health and social care are consistently outperforming both public sector and private sector counterparts when it comes to patient feedback ratings, staff engagement and service user feedback, national patient surveys and financial performance.'*[19]

The *4th Sector* is also remarkably innovative. As SEUK notes, *'The number of social enterprises introducing a new product or service in the last 12 months stands at 50% compared to SMEs overall, which is 33%.'*[20]

But It's Not Easy ...

While the *4th Sector* undoubtedly offers a real, vibrant and productive alternative approach, it can often be hard to find a balance between so many competing demands, particularly when it seems that the alternatives are much simpler.

A recent study – *Can prosocial motivation harm entrepreneurs' subjective well-being?*[21] – found that prosocial motivation negatively affects the life satisfaction of social entrepreneurs via increased levels of stress.

At the core of the paper is an argument that the desire to help others while running a social business can lead to entrepreneurs *'pursuing too many activities, which can deplete personal resources that are important in achieving both organisational and personal goals.'*

In other words, being a *4th Sector* entrepreneur can negatively affect your physical and mental health.

This book is focused on laying out some thoughts on how an individual leader might address this conundrum. But first we want to explore a crucial question - so why do people do it? Why do they take on the myriad challenges of being a *4th Sector* entrepreneur? This is the subject of the next chapter.

Summary

Society is faced with a host of what can at times seem insurmountable problems.

Innovation is essential.

Many advocate for the private sector as the way to find solutions, while others promote the role of government and nearly everyone agrees that there is a role for not-for-profits.

We argue, however, for the need to recognise a 4th Sector of the economy, a place where the enterprise of business is mixed with the sense of service of government and the compassion of not-for-profits, to create an exciting space where innovation for social good can thrive.

We believe that this sector is defined as much by the attitude and intent of its leaders as any legal definition.

But being a *4th Sector* entrepreneur is hard. The need to balance returns for all the stakeholders of an organisation is stressful and can seriously impact on the well-being of its leader.

The rest of this book explores how – as an individual leader – you can address this.

Chapter 2
The Uniqueness Of 4th Sector Entrepreneurs

Introduction

In this chapter we look to get a better sense of the people behind the label of *4th Sector* entrepreneurs. How they form a distinct leadership group facing distinct issues. How they might not only differ from traditional entrepreneurs but also from other leaders in the public or charitable sectors; and how this in turn might influence the way they can successfully negotiate their lives in a healthy and productive way.

What Does It Mean To Be A 4th Sector Entrepreneur?

It's lonely being an entrepreneur - but it's even lonelier being a *4th Sector* entrepreneur!

Entrepreneurs have to focus on only one thing – making money. *4th Sector* entrepreneurs always have to focus on two – money and social value.

Entrepreneurs have a universally agreed way of keeping score, of measuring success – accounting, established over 500 years ago. *4th Sector* entrepreneurs can use accounting but must also struggle with the multitude of ways of measuring social impact, none of which are as clear cut or as universally accepted.

Not only that, they then have to pay two sets of auditors for the privilege of getting them to sign off two reports – their financial accounts and their social impact report.

When someone asks you what you do as an entrepreneur it's simple to answer – I do this to make money. As a *4th Sector* entrepreneur the chances are they will have fallen asleep by the time you start to explain your *Theory of Change* or the assumptions that go into your *Social Value Index*.

When an entrepreneur asks someone to invest money the transaction is simple, the options for an investor to exit long established and easy to compare with other options. A *4th Sector* entrepreneur has to balance all the various stake-holders, starting by educating the representatives of capital who have to get their heads around a whole new way of thinking.

When you ask an entrepreneur about *exit* it's easy to talk about selling for a multiple of earnings and walking away with a pocket full of money as a reward for all the hard work and sacrifices. When you ask a *4th Sector* entrepreneur, such terminology is often considered to be off-limits, obscured by a feeling of guilt, the need to protect vulnerable people and to live up to the original inspiration.

If someone is lucky, all the 70-hour weeks - the grit and determination and financial and emotional sacrifices essential to build any enterprise - might generate a little bit of money and maybe a few awards. But as a wise man once asked us, *Why would anyone choose this path?*

When we set up *Bubble Chamber* as a *4th Sector* enterprise, we had a hypothesis that we could help leaders of other *4th Sector* enterprises gain the clarity and courage they needed to grow their social impact.

So, who are these people we thought we could help? What motivated them to become *4th Sector* entrepreneurs in the first place? Why didn't they choose a *sensible* way of life?

Over the years we have developed a sense of who they might

be. An instinct that the people who would be interested in what we had to offer had a view of the world that made them distinct from other leaders in the economy.

In the business sector, entrepreneurs operate in a world where money reigns supreme. In the public sector, leadership takes a long view in their aim (we hope) to make the world a better place. While charity leaders exist within a world of strict rules and conditions that limit risk.

The people we came across, however, exhibited a relationship with money that clashed with traditional commercial entrepreneurship; a restlessness that made them ill-suited to the public sector; and a willingness to embrace risk to achieve their aims that clashed with the charity sector.

Our sense was that they were, indeed, unique. But who better to ask than the people on the front line.

Research

We had an idea that just as *4th Sector* enterprise demands its own sector of the economy, *4th Sector* entrepreneurs can and should be recognised as a very particular grouping – as individuals with a shared worldview but one that differs from leaders in business, the public sector and charity. Writing this book gave us the opportunity to begin to test this.

We interviewed a selection of people we admired in the sector and asked them three very simple questions:

1. Why did you choose to become a social entrepreneur?
2. What have been your three biggest challenges/frustrations?
3. What three pieces of advice would you give to someone considering going down the same path?

Their responses to the second two questions have helped inform the key principles we outline in the rest of the book. But it is the answers we received to the first question that have given us a clear context for our whole project. And while our research is by no means definitive, we are confident that it shows a pattern that would stand up to robust scrutiny.

Our conversations highlighted four characteristics shared by everyone in our sample group:

1. A commitment to social justice
2. A strong self-belief that it was possible to do things better
3. A strong desire to control their own destiny
4. A drive to make profit not for personal gain but for reinvestment in their social mission.

Here are some of their answers relating to each characteristic.

Commitment To Social Justice

A strong sense of commitment to social justice, in many cases focused on a specific beneficiary group.

June O'Sullivan (Chief Executive, *London Early Years Foundation* – provides quality childcare services in 37 nurseries across London)

'When I was working as a psychiatric nurse as a single parent I had a bad experience finding a nursery for my son given the hours I was working. It made me think that there must be a better way of enabling someone who wanted to work and become independent.'

Kresse Wesling (Co-Founder *Elvis & Kresse* - crafting reclaimed materials into sustainable luxury lifestyle bags and accessories)

'There is no way I can ever repay what I owe to nature and its people.'

Craig Dearden Phillips (Founder, *Social Club & Social Minds* – a unique business club for leaders who want to grow their impact and are ambitious about social change)

'It started as a response to a series of traumatic events in childhood and early adulthood, which meant I was attracted to working with people who were vulnerable as it made me feel useful and validated. Without these events I doubt I would have become a social entrepreneur.'

Susan Aktemel (Founder, *Homes For Good* – social enterprise letting agency)

'My values were really shaped by my experiences between the ages of 16-21 where I was exposed to other cultures by travelling abroad. Especially important was 9 months I spent in

Germany while at University where I did a lot of research into the Nazis and spent time with a number of Holocaust survivors. This made me more receptive to justice and human kindness.'

Rod Schwartz (Founder and CEO, *ClearlySo* - Europe's leading impact investment bank)

'I didn't really decide at any one point. I just made many slight shifts towards it, driven by a sense of doing something meaningful and ultimately something that my children would be proud of.'

Celia Hodson (Founder, *Hey Girls* - tackles period poverty in the UK)

'Setting up a SE was very personal. Period poverty had great resonance as I had brought my kids up on benefits and found it really hard... and I had an overwhelming need to do something about it. I started teaching adults and I realized I really enjoyed being able to help change the way people felt about themselves'

Andrew Preston (Founder, *Exchange Supplies* - supplies products, information and services to improve and prolong the lives of people who inject drugs)

'I have a strong sense of social justice, I think starting from the experience of failing the 11+ exam and experiencing the social exclusion that *the secondary modern kids* had. And then following a re-assessment (because my parents were middle class and appealed the result) being told I had now passed and was going to grammar school. I knew intuitively that it was unjust and had only happened because my parents had different jobs to my friends who were destined for secondary modern school... I saw nursing and health care as political because inequality drives so many health problems. I moved into working with people who use drugs because they have one of the highest levels of morbidity, mortality and social exclusion of any group.'

Rose Marley (CEO, *SharpFutures* – supports diverse young people into employment in the creative digital and tech sectors)

'Being brought up in Manchester, I always had a sense of civic history and duty. I had a lot of pride in being a Mancunian, with a sense that being brought up in the city I was expected to do something to contribute.'

Niall McShannon (Founder and MD, *CCI Scotland* – empowers individuals to make a tangible contribution to their local communities)

'I was always passionate about social justice so got into social work after I realised the law was primarily about defending the system.'

Lea Esterhuizen (*Founder &Wider* – gives tools to companies to engage directly with workers along their supply chain)

'As a white South African I grew up in the 1980s living in an environment full of social injustice, so the best defense for me was to focus on what I could do. I came to the conclusion that a sustainable society needed strong data – you need to know what's needed and where - so I trained up as a data scientist. My subsequent career focused on designing systems to gather sensitive data from scared populations.'

Jack Farmer (Co-Founder, *LettUs Grow* – designs aeroponic irrigation and control technology for indoor and vertical farms)

'I have had a love of nature and plants since I was five and even then all the news coverage was telling me that everything I cared about was dying.'

Heidi Fisher (Founder, *Make An Impact* - supports organisations to become sustainable, grow, and report on the difference they make in society)

'It's in my DNA. My parents and grandparents have always done something to help the community and society.'

Jonathan Parsons (MD, *Chime* – provides NHS Audiology Services for NHS Devon)

'As a clinician with a passion for delivering what's right for the service and our patients, I learnt very early the importance of fighting for my specialty and that if you are willing to accept a sub-optimal service, you get nowhere.'

Sophi Tranchell (Group CEO, *Divine Chocolate* – first *Fairtrade* chocolate bar aimed at the mass market)

'I came from a family of social activists who were always campaigning and I was very involved in the anti-apartheid movement, which showed the power of the purse to effect change. My faith gave me a strong sense of social justice and that I should call things out, as well as introducing me to a number of very inspiring individuals.'

Matt Stevenson Dodd (Founder, *Trust Impact Ltd* – builds trust through transparent impact journeys)

'I was adopted at seven days old and grew up in a happy, loving family. I have always been motivated by the fact that things could have been very different.'

Lucy Marks (Former CEO, *Compass Wellbeing* – providing community health services to improve quality of life including talking therapies and school nursing)

'I had a passion and vision to focus on the quality of care delivered to local people and a passion to innovate and achieve this.'

Matt Wilson (Founder and CEO, *Fuse Events* – delivers socially responsible, world changing events)

'Like many others, I'm sure, my choice was based on my experiences… I was lucky enough to travel around the world. Quite often I'd be staying in 5-star hotels but regardless of the destination, and even in developed countries, I'd only have to walk a few metres out of the hotel to witness real poverty, homelessness and crime borne out of desperation. The contrast between the experience that I was having, and that of many of the local people, was unbearable. Over time I realised the power of live events and how, bringing like-minded people together, we could fight problems like these together to make real, long-lasting positive change.'

Lucy Findlay (Founder and MD, *Social Enterprise Mark* – international accreditation authority)

'My mother did a lot of volunteering through her church and instilled the same ethos in me to try and make the world a better place.'

Kevin Davis (CEO, *Vine Trust Group* – engages in economic and social regeneration)

'I was born and bred in the Black Country and I'm committed to reforming the system so it is open to all people from all backgrounds in the area. I'm driven by spirit/faith, by wanting to make lives better for young people and increase social mobility.'

Neil Woodbridge (CEO, *Thurrock Lifestyle Solutions CIC* – dedicated to empowering the disabled)

'I was brought up around the caring professions but in big institutions. I have always hated unfairness and I was also impacted by the fact that my second cousin, who had spina bifida, died at the age of eight.

Kathryn Uche (Former CEO, CAYSH providing specialist advise, support and accommodation for vulnerable young people and Director of *CAYSH Enterprises CIC* a *Safeguarding Concierge* service)

'I don't like the commercial sector's grip on delivering public services for shareholder profit and the voluntary sector's limiting beliefs don't best service those most in need either.'

John Montague (Director *Big Issue Invest* – strives to dismantle poverty through creating opportunity for people in poverty)

'I worked in the PLC contracting world and was frustrated about society and how we treated people. Clients only cared about making money. My motivation is treating people properly and giving them an opportunity, not seeing them through a preconceived lens.'

Vinay Nair (CEO and Co-founder, *Lightful* – a technology for good company building digital products and services for the social sector)

'The sense of social injustice drives me. A lot of this comes from my broader family. We have a strong matriarchal line. My grandmothers and grand-aunts were freedom fighters in Kerala and politicians fighting for social justice.'

Poppy Jarman Founder *Mental Health First Aid England*

'I was driven by discrimination right back to childhood. As an Asian woman who experienced both gender and race discrimination, I remember feeling that's not right, I'm going to do something about it.'

Alisha Fernandez Miranda CEO *IG Consulting* and Trustee *B Lab*

'I also had a strong sense of justice - that things should just be fair.'

Doing Things Better

A strong self-belief that it was possible to do things better and that, no matter how difficult, they would figure out some way to make things happen.

Andrew Preston

'I was a harm reduction activist and there were things that needed doing. I decided that as no one else was going to do them, I should - because I could. The products we originally developed were technically illegal to distribute and the company was set up because we couldn't get anyone to supply the products that were needed to prevent drug related harm.'

Lucy Findlay

'I came across a number of community-based regeneration schemes. I saw a particular scheme that had a more sustainable approach at a Welsh Mining community called Ystalyfera, where I met a very inspiring woman. She explained how to set up a Community Development Trust where the regeneration grant was used to invest in assets that created an income and carry on regenerating the community, compared to other projects where the grant was spent and then regeneration finished'

Niall McShannon

'I felt that a person-centred, asset-based approach was the right way to help people.'

Kresse Wesling

'In 2004, I started researching the UK waste situation at the *British Library*. We sent 100 million tonnes of waste to landfill in that year. I went to landfills specifically to get a better understanding of exactly what was ending up there, to see if there was anything I could do. That is when I saw my first fire-hose.'

Brendan Martin (Founder and MD, *Buurtzorg* Britain and Ireland – provides holistic community care through self-managed teams)

'There is manifestly a crisis in home care services, job quality and resource use and I became convinced that our approach could contribute to the solution. I was convinced that small, self-organised neighbourhood teams – operating in flexible, holistic ways that cut out the management layers and inefficiencies that resulted from a command-and-control system – was the way to go. It would enable the front line to apply their vocational commitment, common sense and, to the extent they have it in home care, professional training.'

Lea Esterhuizen

'Business can deliver sustainable impact and businesses, as clients, can also really scale positive impact – if you can harness the opportunities, listen well and engage your clients to help you continuously up your game.'

Gillian Holdsworth (Founder, *SH:24* – provides free and confidential online sexual and reproductive health services 24 hours a day)

'I was brought up in a family where it was always a matter of questioning if something was the best way of doing things and of looking for the next challenge. So I have always been a person who looked for solutions rather than problems. Setting up outside of the process-driven nature of the *NHS* has been incredibly liberating.'

Neil Woodbridge

'In 1996, I wanted to get experience working in local government, so applied to Thurrock. Over time I came to believe that we could do this better ourselves and so we developed a user-run approach, where we moved from people being passive recipients of care to active citizens in control.'

Rose Marley

'My mum, who was widowed at 31 and left to bring up three small kids, went on to get an *Open University* degree and had a very successful career. She always told us there was no such thing as *can't*.'

David Schluter (Founder, *Fluid IT* – offers tailored IT support)

'I was outraged to see charities being mis-sold IT solutions. I was then offered the opportunity by one of the charities I was supporting to re-train ex-offenders on the job and my faith compelled me to try.'

Gina Rowlands (MD, *Bevan Healthcare* – offers an integrated GP model of health and wellbeing within primary care for the homeless, asylum seekers and refugees)

'I believe that all nurses have the potential to be entrepreneurial and change the way services are delivered'

Jo Morrell

'I wanted other people to experience volunteering and community in the way that I have experienced. I wanted to share that feeling.'

Rod Schwartz

'I was the Chair of a large national charity which I found inefficient, bureaucratic, with poor governance and focused on its own existence rather than creating impact - so I quit. At the same time I became Chair of a company called *Just Giving,* which was making an impact by channelling money to charities (it raised over $6 billion over time) and was disruptive. It reduced the cost of giving money to charity from 23% to 5%, and looked likely to be very successful as a business (investors made twenty times their money). So I thought I could use my skills to create a hundred businesses like it.'

Ben Lane (*Acumen Academy UK* – seeks to change the way the world tackles poverty by investing in sustainable businesses, leaders and ideas)

'I was driven by an interest in the power of market forces to solve problems of poverty.'

Controlling Their Destiny

A strong desire to control their own destiny, often arising from a frustration with hierarchy and bureaucracy and the courage to take a risk to follow this through.

June O'Sullivan

'Working within the Local Authority limits you at every level…. they are so slow it does your head in.'

Jack Farmer

'Business was also ideal for bringing people together behind a desire to do something positive as opposed to the charity/ protest sectors which tend to be about opposition.'

Susan Aktemel

'I rejected the idea of being a charity or a limited company as I wanted to be completely accountable for making the money I needed to survive.'

Kresse Wesling

'I had nothing to lose so I decided to set up my own company ... I would rather fail at doing something spectacularly good than carry on in a job which was associated with all kinds of destructive processes ... I think that entrepreneurship is an interesting option for new arrivals. I didn't know the business landscape in the UK or what kinds of companies might hire me. In a way it was easier to start something myself.'

Lucy Marks

'When the opportunity to spin out came up, I already had that mindset - so it seemed obvious. In fact, it seemed riskier to me to stay within the system. I would have just got bored, because it would have been so difficult to create the changes that needed to be made. My view was if we screw up, at least it will be our own fault.'

Ben Rick (Founder and MD, SASC – funds organisations that support communities and improve people's lives)

'I would never have considered myself to be an entrepreneur and it's only recently that I've admitted it – begrudgingly. I was always comfortable being a cog in a big organisation. In fact, I liked it more than working in a smaller organisation. So, I was never desperate to set up my own business.

But I now realise that I enjoy running a small business, above all the ability to be guided by my own belief system.'

Gina Rowlands

'We were a small general practice with a unique cohort of patients. They are often described as *hard to reach*. We take the view, they are easy to ignore. The unwieldy bureaucratic system of the NHS re-enforced this view. It was incredibly frustrating and demoralising for the staff and patients.'

Nial McShannon

'I found it very frustrating to work in a system where outputs were imposed, with the best intentions, by the bureaucracy. I realised that the best way to go was to do it myself.'

Illana Taub (Co-Founder, *SNACT* – makes wholesome snacks to create more taste and less waste)

'I saw my role in making the world a better place as being in business and to this day can't see an alternative route.'

Tom Kay (Founder, *Finisterre* – designs functional and sustainable products for sea-lovers)

'I have always forged my own way.'

Neil Woodbridge

'People in local government often describe me as a maverick.'

Vinay Nair

'When I stepped across from a non-exec role to be CEO of *Lightful*, I was really attracted by the opportunity to shape something. I get energy from others and really enjoy team-building as well as having the chance to change things.'

Dai Powell (CEO, HCT Group – provides bus services, social services transport, school buses, minibuses and more across the UK)

'I liked *having a go* and I thought this offered an exciting opportunity to do a lot more differently and better.'

Profit for Reinvestment

A drive and enjoyment of making profit, not for personal gain but for reinvestment in their social mission.

Sophi Tranchell

'I was entrepreneurial from a young age and used to buy bread and bring a toaster to school to make toast to sell - but I was never interested in making money for money's sake. I was much more interested in how it could be used for good.'

Andrew Croft (CE, *CAN* – provides premises, finance and skills for the Third Sector)

'I had seen enough of *shareholder value* and came across the concept of social enterprise, which was an opportunity to run a business for the stakeholders, not the shareholders.'

Rose Marley

'When I got pregnant with my first child I started to ask myself what kind of world was I bringing my child into and whether there was a better way to earn a living than running after celebrities in the music business.'

Ben Rick

'I wanted to challenge the idea that wealth could only be created for one person at the expense of everyone else. Having worked for so long in a business where success was all about money I wanted to show that it was possible to make money in a fair way.'

Jonathan Parsons

'Becoming a social enterprise gave us a certainty of budget and crucially the opportunity to reinvest our own money in making the service better for the patients.'

Karen Lynch (CEO, *Belu Water* – supplies low carbon-footprint water to the hotel, restaurant and catering sector)

'My family would always say I was an entrepreneur. I think I had my first car-wash business at eight and I was always making things to sell. I wasn't motivated by money though. I just like making people happy and from an early age really hated waste.'

Neil Woodbridge

'My wife thinks I'm not earning enough but I think I'm paid too much.'

Matt Stevenson Dodd

'I needed to do something that was entrepreneurial but never wanted just to make money for other people.'

Lea Esterhuizen

'I worked in the international development space but didn't want to rely on donor funding as donors can change their minds on funding priorities, which makes cash flow unreliable. I felt I had an obligation to address this and at the same time ensure we were not donor-reliant and could sustain our growth and impact over time.'

Tom Kay

'From the beginning I wanted the brand to have a wider remit than just existing as a business; to stand for something and have a real purpose. We have always stood for three points of commitment - people, product and the environment - and I wanted to inspire people to have a relationship with the sea.'

David Schluter

'I didn't want to make rich people richer.'

Summary

In this chapter we considered the uniqueness of the *4th Sector* entrepreneur.

We reflected on the difficulties they face in serving two masters – money and social impact.

We then presented a hypothesis of the key characteristics of these entrepreneurs, developed through our experience and then tested through a series of interviews we undertook with current leaders in the sector.

We summarised our conclusion by defining four key characteristics and illustrated them through direct quotes from our interviews:

1. An active commitment to social justice.
2. A strong self-belief that it was possible to do things better.
3. A strong desire to control their own destiny.
4. A drive to make profit not for personal gain but for reinvestment in their social mission.

The next section of the book considers how to lay the groundwork for addressing the challenges these create.

Part 2
Laying The Foundations

Part 2
Introduction To Laying The Foundations

We passionately believe that the foundation of your well-being as a leader is being able to work on your business rather than in it. It's being able to rise above day-to-day tactics and develop the strategies you need to leverage all your assets in the service of creating social value.

That's why we've called this part *Laying the Foundations.*

In it you'll find valuable suggestions on how you can successfully extricate yourself from the pressure of feeling that you have to deal with everything and develop a more effective way of working, one that will drive your organisation forward.

Chapter 3 explains a simple but powerful model called *The 4Cs Formula*. This is a virtuous circle that starts with your *Commitment,* which prompts your *Courage* to do whatever is necessary to develop your *Capability,* which helps you become more *Confident,* which deepens your *Commitment* – and so on.

Chapter 4 addresses *Personal Productivity.* It looks at giving up trying to manage time and focusing instead on managing stress and your energy.

Finally, in this part, Chapter 5 explores good habits and how to develop them, so that you can maximise the value from implementing everything that follows.

Chapter 3
The 4 Cs

'High Impact Entrepreneurs stick to it for longer.'

Rod Schwartz, Founder and CEO, *ClearlySo*

Introduction

Why do some people go from success to success while others never seem to get going?

What's stood out from every interview we've had with successful *4th Sector* entrepreneurs is their strong commitment to social justice, which gives them a willingness to take risks that others may have questioned. So many have talked about how they have experienced fear, uncertainty and discomfort but happily working through it due to their commitment to their overall goal.

Dan Sullivan of *Strategic Coach,* a highly successful company that helps entrepreneurs grow their businesses, has spent over forty years coaching entrepreneurs and has developed a theory that backs this up.

He calls this *The 4Cs Formula.*

What Does The 4Cs Formula Look Like?

Sullivan describes *The 4Cs* as a four-stage clockwise progression, as illustrated below:

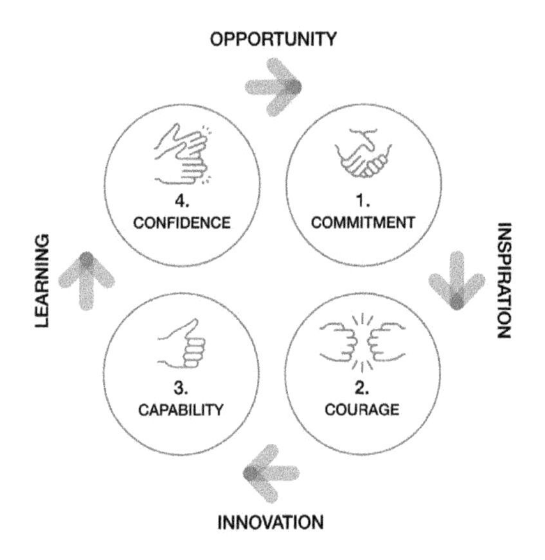

Figure 3.1 The 4Cs Formula (courtesy of Strategic Coach)

The starting point is for an individual to make a commitment to achieve a specific measurable result by a specific date in the future.

This commitment requires a level of courage to move forward, as it means someone often has to take action before they have the capability to achieve that result.

Once they're courageous to make that first step though, the necessary capability soon follows which in turn breeds confidence.

It's simple.

Exercise

Remember something that you are proud of having achieved where you feel you took a big jump in capability and confidence as a result of having gone through the experience.

Now take a piece of paper and draw four boxes as below.

We suggest filling the whole page. At the top of the page write down the name of what you did and the date when it happened.

4 C's Model Exercise

Title: ______________________ Date: ______________

OPPORTUNITY

4. My new higher CONFIDENCE...	1. What I COMMITTED to
3. The CAPABILITY that emerged	3. Why this took COURAGE

LEARNING

INSPIRATION

INNOVATION

Now take ten minutes to fill in the boxes as follows:

- Write down the commitment you made to yourself at the time
- Describe the courage it required on your part to move forward on that commitment
- Identify the new capability that emerged as a result
- Write down the new level of confidence you achieved as a result and what that produced

If you can, now share what you have written with someone else who you think could also benefit from doing the same exercise.

Why Is Commitment First?

Without a strong, specific commitment it's enormously difficult to get started at all.

Sullivan describes commitment as something that's created when you make a sale to yourself. In other words, it requires you selling yourself on doing something that you don't feel you have the capability to pull off.

As he says, 'We often talk about sales in terms of selling to someone else but actually the first sale that you have to make to advance… is to sell yourself on a goal… to intellectually engage… with a future desirable result beyond your capability.'

The commitment stage is all about stating a particular result. When you do this you immediately move into the *Courage* phase - what you need in order to address all the fears and worries that making this commitment immediately creates.

'Just do it. It won' be perfect from the start and you don't know what you need to know until you start.'

Ilana Taub, Co-Founder, *Snact*

What Is Courage?

When faced with the possibility of failure, especially when in a position of responsibility, we all experience fear - but we all have a choice on how to respond.

Courage can be defined as the willingness to go forward even though you don't feel confident about success and are tempted to procrastinate and stop.

Sullivan talks about courage as a skill rather than an emotion and therefore something that he believes anyone can develop. And while exercising courage is something that doesn't always feel comfortable, he emphasises that it's essential if you're going to increase your capability in order to achieve a higher level of confidence. Courage creates a rush of adrenaline that puts your brain on high alert, which in turn sharpens your sense of urgency, simplifying your priorities and decisions and giving you the energy to move forward.

Crucially, it's also a key stimulant for creativity because, as Sullivan notes, 'Innovation occurs in the dynamic zone between courage and capability. The moment you take that risk for the sake of something bigger and better your brain becomes creative, innovative and inventive.'

Capability Creates Confidence

So being courageous - with a clear commitment to a goal – drives the energy to innovate and develop new, more powerful capabilities. At which point it's inevitable that your confidence will jump.

These capabilities can cover a variety of areas - personal, team, funding – but in essence what they mean is that you're now able to do something today and in the future that you couldn't do in the past. That you have confidence in your ability to deliver. A sense of certainty and calmness that you can achieve your goal.

Beware though, confidence can easily create complacency.

When you feel good about things there is always the temptation to enjoy yourself and relax. It's so often seen in the sporting world, where an individual or team wins something big and then loses the commitment to continue to develop. Inevitably, someone else comes through to beat them.

The only way to combat this is to go on to make a bigger commitment that puts your confidence at risk. That's why Sullivan talks about *The 4Cs* as a *closed loop*, where it's crucial to keep flexing each muscle – commitment, courage, capability and confidence – to keep things moving forward. As we shall see in the next chapter, continual development is all about looking for more resistance and a bigger challenge.

Your Job As The Chief Commitment Officer

The 4Cs are not something that you can delegate.

In leading your organisation, you become the role model for everyone else, so when it comes to *The 4Cs* this effectively makes you the *Chief Commitment Officer.* When you're seen to commit yourself totally to something, everyone else is encouraged to do the same. By the same token, if you're not seen to be committing, nobody else will be willing to either.

Likewise, your courage gives everyone else the courage to take risks without a guarantee of success.

For Sullivan, taking this approach makes leadership pretty simple – your job as leader is to *continually make commitment, courage, capability and confidence the fundamental philosophy that drives growth.*

Simple - but difficult to achieve. Particularly when faced with the never-ending pressure of day-to-day management. That's why in the next chapter we consider another foundation stone of well-being – personal productivity.

Exercise

Take 15 minutes to write down as many situations as you can think of where you feel you have made a breakthrough in your life – either personal or at work.

In how many did your mindset follow *The Formula?*

Summary

This chapter describes a simple model for effective leaderships called *The 4Cs Formula.*

Your first step as leader to make a *Commitment* to a clearly defined goal, no matter how scared this makes you feel.

This requires *Courage* – the willingness to go forward before you're confident that you have the capability to reach that goal.

Being courageous will drive the creativity and innovation that you need to build your *Capability,* which will in turn build your *Confidence* to move forward and make the next *Commitment.*

As *Chief Commitment Officer* it's a cycle of growth that you have to live, not delegate.

'It's never going to be perfect. So get in the habit of starting things that are 7/10 rather than waiting for everything to be 10/10.'

Tom Kay, Founder, *Finisterre*

'Be resilient, flexible and confident.

Treasure the serendipitous.... things don't usually go according to plan but don't be down hearted as this often leads to something good as long as you can be flexible.

Have the confidence to go off-piste but keep asking the question does this add value to the core?'

June O'Sullivan, Chief Executive, *London Early Years Foundation*

Get uncomfortable - it is always difficult to get out of your comfort zone, but it is the place the learning happens. Building your growth mindset, and experiments to explore your limits and fail safely, asking yourself each day 'how do I want to show up?' and 'what's the worst thing that can happen?

Ben Lane, *Acumen Academy UK*

Chapter 4
Personal Productivity

'Never lose site of why you decided to do it in the first place. If you find it doesn't inspire you then stop!'

Ben Rick, Founder and MD, *SASC*

Introduction

How often have you heard someone say, 'I am so stressed – because I just don't have enough time?'

When it comes to growing your social impact, we couldn't agree more. For the busy social entrepreneur, time is usually the crucial thing that's in short supply. Too many things to do, and never enough time to do them.

Result? Pressure, opportunities lost, corners cut (maybe). And stress (definitely).

So, if time really is your most valuable commodity, it makes sense to reflect on how you might go about using it in the most productive ways possible. Specifically, this means reviewing the time you spend working on your business rather than in it; working on the systems that guide and enable growth, rather than on fire-fighting.

Why You Need To Give Up Trying To Manage Time

Isn't the obvious solution simply to manage your time better? No. Alistair Lobo[22] – a specialist in helping leaders increase their productivity – recommends another approach, developed from a best-selling book called *The Power of Full Engagement* by Tony Schwartz. "While Jules Verne and Marty and Doc in *Back to the Future* could manage time, the reality is that we mere humans can't," says Lobo.

"Being personally productive is not about managing time but about managing the energy that comes from stress. Key to this is being able to differentiate between healthy or *eustress* and unhealthy *distress*."

As we discussed in *The 4Cs Formula*, stress is vital for the creative process. But it's also vital to avoid *over-stress*, as that's when your energy disappears and you stop getting things done. Lobo used the metaphor of a bodybuilder to illustrate his point.

"No-one walks into a gym and immediately bench-presses twice their bodyweight. If they try, at best they will not even move the bar and at worst they will do themselves some damage. Once they commit to a goal, they start with a much smaller weight that puts their muscles under stress but which they can lift and then every few days add another 5lbs.

In between sessions in the gym they rejuvenate, they sleep, they consider their nutrition and then, when their body has healed, come back. After many cycles the weight they couldn't move can now be lifted with ease.

The same principle holds true when it comes to being more productive in managing your life. You can't expect to juggle everything without a plan to manage the stress."

And so, give up even thinking about trying to manage time. The key to personal productivity is to embrace that old enemy stress as a friend, celebrating its benefits but also managing it systematically and incrementally, in a positive way, to ensure you maximise your energy.

Easy for us to say! To help you achieve this, here are some practical suggestions.

Exercise

Give yourself a mark out of 10 for how much stress lack of time causes you, both at work and in your personal life. Now think of two areas where, if you addressed them, you could reduce this stress level by 2 points.

Where Do You Start?

With identification. You have to ask yourself a very basic question – how productive am I now? And we're not talking guesswork here. You need to look, as objectively as you can, at the reality of where you're currently putting your effort. The process is quite straightforward – but it needs you to be honest and disciplined in recording what you do.

First you need to draw the simple time management matrix that was designed by Stephen Covey[23] in his great book, *The 7 Habits of Highly Effective People (see Fig 4.1):*

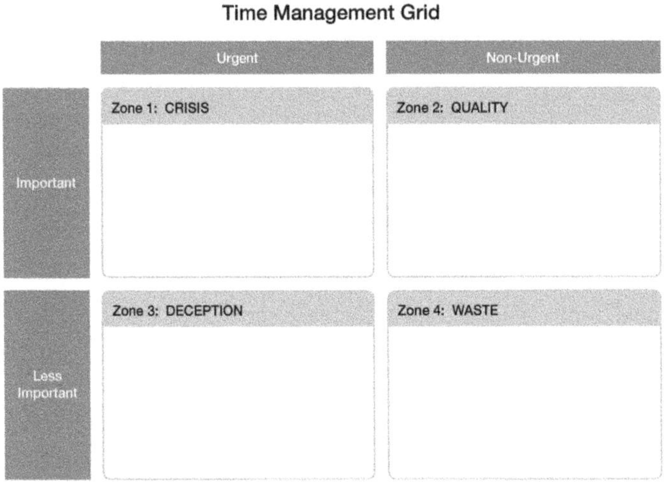

Time Management Grid

	Urgent	Non-Urgent
Important	Zone 1: CRISIS	Zone 2: QUALITY
Less Important	Zone 3: DECEPTION	Zone 4: WASTE

Figure 4.1: Steven Covey's Time Management Matrix from *The 7 Habits of Highly Effective People*

Zone 1 relates to the urgent and important – pressing problems, deadlines, crises even. Making effort here is unavoidable but we need to ask how many of these demands have become urgent through procrastination, insufficient planning, poor communication and a whole host of other possible factors.

Zone 2 is where we do long-range development; we anticipate and prevent problems by using *Plan-Do-Review* methodology (more on that later); we increase our skills and knowledge; and we invest in relationships using our core communication habits. Making effort here increases our ability to get things done before they become urgent. So it also shrinks *Zone 1*.

Zone 3 is the *Zone of Deception* because the noise of urgency creates the illusion of importance – but for whom? If we're not careful we can spend a lot of time and effort here in meeting the priorities of other people.

And *Zone 4*? Well, we tend to go here simply to escape from *Zones 1* and *3* – and we don't get anything done that's productive. At all.

Now, the key point here is research shows conclusively that:

People who use their time most effectively
spend the vast majority of it in Zone 2.

This is the main generator of productivity. Double your *Zone 2* score and you will probably halve the time spent fire-fighting in *Zone 1* and quadruple the success of your enterprise at the same time.

Exercise
Identify Your Personal Productivity Score

So, taking the matrix, do the following:

1. Quick subjective estimate. What percentage of your time – both at work and away from it – do you think you spend in each of the four zones, especially *Zone 2*?
2. A more objective analysis – *Personal Productivity Score.* Over the next three days – at least two of which must be work days – keep a diary of how you spend your time. Set the alarm on your phone or watch to go off every hour that you are aware and write down what you have been doing, under the four zone headings. At the end of three days calculate what percentage of time you have actually spent in each zone and compare the results of the two exercises. The figure in *Zone 2* represents your *Personal Productivity Score.*

How MOSES Can Help You Increase Your Personal Productivity Score?

MOSES is a five-step process, created by Alistair Lobo, that has been proven to increase personal productivity. It stands for:

- **M**indset – your basic attitude to, and understanding of, how you work
- **O**utcomes – identifying the outcomes that are important to you and what you need to do to achieve them
- **S**trategies – defining the 'how', the actions that will make you more productive
- **E**xecution – consistently doing the strategies effectively
- **S**kills – stands for investing in the skills and knowledge you need to keep improving.

MINDSET: Why Is It First?

Mindset comes first because challenging the way you think about how you work is the most basic – and most important – hurdle you have to overcome if you're going to radically improve your personal productivity.

'I have too much to do to stop and think…'

'I'm the only one that can do this…'

'I have to answer every email immediately…'

So where should you start? Well, what this comes down to – practically – is two things.

1. Reality - seeing the reality of how you work now i.e. your Personal Productivity Score.
2. Myths - slaying any myths you might be buying into, unconsciously perhaps, that are holding you back. Beliefs that form the premise on which you build your daily routine.

Put the two together – seeing reality and slaying the myths – and your current mindset is going to get a serious jolt.

OUTCOMES:
How Can You Identify The Important Ones?

How can you shift your focus from the *Urgent* to the *Important*, from *Zones 1* and *3* to *Zone 2*? How can you know what are the important outcomes for you? It comes down to two things:

1. Clarity of your role in your *4th Sector* enterprise
2. Clarity of the *purpose, vision and values* of that role

How Can You Clarify Your Roles?

If someone asked you to describe yourself, what would you say? You might start by talking about your age, your gender, where you're from. Pretty soon you'd get on to what you do and the various roles you play – at work, in your family, in your social group and, more broadly, in how you relate to society as a whole.

A lot of stress can come from the conflicting demands these various roles impose on us – work versus family versus spending time with our friends versus, say, volunteering. So, being fully conscious of all the roles we play – and how we prioritise them – can help us to clarify what is important to us. Which, in turn, can help us address and manage the stress and conflict we might be experiencing.

So, what are your roles – all of them? Make a quick list and put a percentage figure against each one that indicates how much of your time you spend in that particular role.

How Can You Identify What Is Important For Each Role?

When you've clarified each role, how can you shift your focus from the *Urgent* to the *Important* - from *Zones 1* and *3* to *Zone 2* – in each role? How can you know what are the important outcomes for you? And what can you do if you've got your day all carefully planned… and someone comes to you with a *drop-everything-really-urgent* need?

The key to this is being clear about the following:

- The *Purpose* of the role – for example, in your *4th Sector* entrepreneur role, what service and value does it provide for which customer or end-user, what problem does it solve for them? If you're clear about this, it's so much easier to see whether or not a particular task or activity directly serves that purpose and therefore how it should be prioritised.

- The *Values* of the role – the things that define and guide your emotional behaviour in handling the situation.
- The *Vision* for the role – how it fits in the bigger picture? If I had to describe it to someone in a lift what would I say? What story would I tell?
- My short-term *Goals* for the role? – what is the one thing that I am aiming to do in this role in the next week that will have the greatest positive impact.

We'll look at *Purpose, Vision and Values* and the clarity of your goals in more detail later on in the book. For now, it's sufficient simply to recognise the important role they play in acting as a kind of filter to differentiate between what is *Urgent (Zone 1)* and what is *Important (Zone 2)*. Then it's simply a question of applying the old 80:20 rule:

Take the top 20% of what is important and dedicate 80% of your time to getting it done.

Few people get anywhere near 80% in the real world but with every bit of progress you make in that direction, your days become more productive and the whole organisation benefits as a result.

STRATEGIES: What Key Ones Do You Need To Achieve Your Goals?

Once you've defined what is important to you and the specific goals you want to achieve, how do you go about realising them? What practical actions do you need to take to become more productive, more effective?

One way is to develop strategies in four key areas - mental, physical, emotional and spiritual. Take action, bit by bit, in each area and you will be surprised at the progress you're able to make. Let's look at each area in turn.

A *mental strategy* means working out how to think clearly about what you need to do to achieve your goals. Alistair Lobo recommends something called *The D Method*. This involves you every day writing down a list of things you have to do and then applying one of four *Ds*. So you either:

- *DO* it straight away, particularly if it's something you can do in one or two minutes.
- *DIARISE* it i.e. you set a definite date for when you're actually going to do it.
- *DELEGATE* it i.e. you think 'I'm going to get that person to do it' as they're capable or even best suited to doing it well. (We cover this in more detail in the chapter on *Talent Strategy*, where we consider the importance of you as leader having the right people in the right place at the right time.)
- *DUMP* it or *DELETE* it – because it's not relevant to any of your goals.

By consistently writing things down and addressing the list every day in this way, the mental clutter in your head will disappear because your brain knows that you're going to follow through on these decisions.

A *physical strategy* means making a plan to ensure you have the physical well-being to be able to do effectively what you need to do. Taking regular exercise so that you have enough physical energy is key not just for your physical well-being but your emotional well-being, too.

Your *emotional strategy*, meanwhile, helps you develop the emotional resilience you need to handle life's challenges, build strong relationships and recover from setbacks.

Not surprisingly, because we're human beings, not robots, all of these aspects of our lives – physical, emotional and mental – are interlinked. And this is where a *spiritual strategy* can help, too, because this could be described as how you tie everything together; how you find meaning in life's events, demonstrate your unique purpose and develop the ability to be compassionate towards others.

Now, exactly what form that spiritual strategy can take varies hugely from person to person. For some it can be a religious practice; for others mindfulness or meditation; or keeping a gratitude journal; or long walks in the countryside – or even just gardening. There are lots of possibilities. The point is to find something that helps you reflect and gather a sense of wholeness and perspective.

So, bottom line, in each of these four areas – mental, physical, emotional and spiritual – it really helps to make a plan, a strategy.

EXECUTION:
What Does Executing Your Strategies Involve?

The E in the acronym *MOSES* stands for *Execution* – that is, executing or carrying out your strategies. Which means, obviously, that you have to take the action to turn them into reality.

So, if your mental strategy is *The D-Method* – Execute it! That is, *Do it, Delegate it, Diarise it* or *Delete it.* Simple. And if your physical strategy calls for you to take a vigorous, 20-minute walk every day – well, take a vigorous twenty- minute walk every day. What's stopping you?

Actually, it could be quite a lot, because to become more productive you have to turn your strategy into hard-wired, consistent behaviour over time, which usually means confronting some kind of resistance, such as unlearning or replacing other forms of ingrained behaviour along the way. Habits, in other words. And everyone knows how difficult that can be.

But only recently have researchers discovered exactly why

– neural pathways. These are information fast-tracks that we create in the brain through doing, which then help shape how we think. The next chapter looks in more detail at habits and how to embed the behaviour that you've identified to make you more productive; as Steven Covey states as his seventh habit - *Sharpen The Saw*.

SKILLS: Why Is It Important To Invest In Developing Them?

It's a cliché to say that the world is constantly changing – and it's changing at an ever-increasing rate. But that means that if you're not constantly changing with it – constantly developing, learning and growing, 'sharpening the saw' – you're not standing still but actually going backwards, falling behind while the world charges on. And probably taking your enterprise backwards with you.

That's why the last letter of MOSES stands for *Skills*, which also includes *Knowledge* and *Wisdom*. In short, it stands for a personal development strategy that helps you grow in all three areas.

Knowledge is what is already understood about something. Your challenge is to absorb that understanding yourself – to learn it – in a way that's best for you. This could be by reading, doing online or conventional courses, listening to podcasts – whatever fits your lifestyle and how you learn best.

Skills are developed by doing, by putting your knowledge into action, applying it. So again, you need a strategy that pushes you to develop different skills in different situations.

And Wisdom comes from observing and reflecting on the results of how your knowledge and skills have been applied to particular challenges. So your strategy needs to allow space for lessons not only to be identified, but crucially, to be learnt, so that past mistakes aren't simply noted, then repeated.

In summary, whether you call it continuous professional

development or continuous personal development, and whether you see it as an investment in your enterprise or in yourself, learning and developing your expertise in the areas you've defined as important is essential. And if it's adding to the value you can create in the world it can even be experienced as a pleasure rather than a chore.

Recapping MOSES

So that's MOSES. *Mindset* – your basic attitude to, and understanding of, how you work; *Outcomes* – identifying the outcomes that are important to you and what you need to do to achieve them; *Strategies* – defining the how, the actions that will make you more productive; *Execution* – consistently doing the strategies effectively; and *Skills* – for investing in the skills, knowledge and wisdom you need to keep improving. Apply it consistently and your personal productivity could go through the roof.

However, as the poet Robbie Burns once famously observed, T*he best laid schemes o' mice an' men/Gang aft a-gley*; which roughly translates as *things don't always turn out as you planned*.

So, what then?

How Do You Deal With The Unexpected?

Imagine you're the skipper of a small boat, sailing across a wide, unpredictable sea. You know where you're headed, everything is organised and planned to the nearest detail. BUT you never know exactly what the wind is going to do, or the weather. Storms can blow up suddenly, out of nowhere. Which is why, whatever happens, you know you've to rely on your compass and your maps. In any situation, they are your ultimate reference point.

Well, it's sometimes said that running a *4th Sector* enterprise is a bit like skippering a boat.

There are certainly stormy days and days of calm – even days of plain sailing. But throughout, what do you use for a compass, and a map – the ultimate points of reference?

As we shall see in Chapters 7 and 8, they have to be your personal and your enterprise's *Purpose, Vision and Values.* Because however effective you are at organising your time and focusing on the important, and however personally productive you are, you can never know or control in advance everything that's going to happen. But if you've internalised your enterprise's *Purpose, Vision and Values,* ensuring they are congruent with your own, you will be able to respond with confidence to any specific moment, any specific demand, by referring with integrity to this *inner compass.*

So, practically, how do you set this *inner compass?*

A simple first step is to develop the habit of always previewing the day – spending a few minutes at the beginning of the day (or last thing before you go to bed) to look over your schedule and check it against:

- the four Zones of *Crisis, Quality, Deception* and *Waste.*
- your overall *Purpose, Vision and Values.*

In that way, not only will your schedule align as far as possible with what is most important to your enterprise's core purpose, but when the unexpected crops up – as it will – your thinking, decisions and responses will already be set to bring things back on course.

The Pause: A Powerful Tool For Productivity

The pause is a powerful tool for productivity. So, what is it and how can it help? Consider these three scenarios.

- *Scenario 1* – A critic of Boss A's social enterprise says something ill-informed about it on *Twitter*. Boss A is exasperated – this loud-mouthed ignoramus is causing trouble again – and immediately responds with a tweet putting the critic straight.
- *Scenario 2* – Boss B is involved in a long and detailed planning meeting when she gets a text from her biggest customer, furious that a delivery hasn't arrived. She hurries out of the meeting to make a soothing phone call before trying to sort things out.
- *Scenario 3* – Boss C is about to leave work early to be home in time for a family event, when he gets a call from a customer – she's furious that a delivery hasn't arrived and demands that he sorts it out. Boss C promises to deal with it – but heads off home. This customer is always making trouble and the problem can wait.

Three scenarios, three bosses, three decisions. And all different – except for one thing. In each case, the boss was confronted with something unexpected – and simply reacted. With an angry *Tweet* in *Scenario 1*, and an instant decision to attend to a demanding customer in *Scenario 2* or ignore her in *Scenario 3*.

Now, it's impossible to say whether each decision was right or wrong – we don't have enough information. But what is clear is that each decision would have benefited from *The Pause* – the ability to increase the space between the initial stimulus and the response to it. In fact, it's *The Pause* that marks the difference between a reaction – something instant, habitual and often quite emotional – and a response, which is basically more considered.

The Pause allows you to really *listen* to a stimulus – whatever it is – and then connect with your *Purpose, Vision and Values*, so you can ask yourself:

- 'What is the best use of my time right now based on these key elements and the 4Ds?'
- 'Is this issue important or simply urgent – or neither?'
- 'Would it be consistent with my *Purpose, Vision and Values* if I said I'm busy and arranged another specific time to address the issue?'

Experience shows that by using *The Pause* and responding to the situation – based on *Purpose, Vision and Values* – we're more likely to find the courage and wisdom to make the best decision for everyone than if we simply and instantly react.

How Do You Measure Your Productivity Gains?

So how are you doing? It's a question you need to ask yourself regularly if you're going to take your personal productivity seriously. But let's be honest – it's also just one of a multitude of things you have to juggle as a busy CEO and evaluating your own performance might seem a bit too much like navel-gazing if you spend a lot of time on it.

How do you find the right balance then?

One way is to set regular, rough-and-ready evaluation points – every week or month, say – so the period just gone can be used as the basis for your increased effectiveness in the period coming up. For example, at the end of every week, you might ask yourself:

- What goals did I achieve?
- What challenges did I encounter?
- What difficult decisions did I make? And in making them, how often did I use the compass of my *Purpose, Vision and Values* rather than my emotions – or the clock?
- And then you could ask yourself, what can I do to improve things next week?

So that's the ongoing, regular evaluation. But then, at least once – or maybe twice – a year you can revisit the process outlined in the earlier part on how to calculate your current personal productivity. This is a more structured process that needs you to monitor your activity in a disciplined and thought-out framework, a bit like your annual accounts or stocktaking.

Every 6-12 months you need to look again at the four Zones relating to *Urgent, Non-Urgent, Important* and *Less Important* activity, how much time you spend in each zone, and then calculate your subjective and objective productivity. Have you improved, flat-lined – or even gone backwards?

And of course, there is one other way of evaluating your performance – you can ask people. Your colleagues, your customers, your suppliers, even your friends and family can give you valuable feedback - if you've got a thick enough skin…

Summary

Improving your personal productivity comes from under-standing that it's not possible to manage time. What you can manage is your levels of stress, which directly link to your energy levels and so impact on your levels of productivity.

This change of attitude starts by reframing the problem, by accepting that stress is natural and important for growth and – as we talked about in *The 4Cs* model in Chapter 3 – you arguably need it to drive you forward.

Your biggest enemy, then, is not being stressed but being over-stressed to the point where you're no longer able to recover, your energy dips and you stop being productive. That means you need to learn how to manage stress effectively in order to maximise your personal productivity.

To do this begin by identifying, then prioritising and finally executing, the things that are important for the roles you fulfil in your professional and personal life.

Measure how productive you are at the moment and then use the *MOSES* five-step approach to improve things in a systematic way.

It's a straightforward approach. It requires commitment and courage but also a willingness to do the work to develop some important habits. We'll look at some tips on how to do this in the next chapter.

'Sometimes it is crucial to do nothing and then solutions and ideas emerge more easily.'

Lea Esterhuizen, Founder *&Wilder*

Chapter 5
Habits And How To Develop Them

'Change might not be fast and it isn't always easy. But with time and effort, almost any habit can be reshaped.'

Charles Duhigg, *The Power of Habit: Why We Do What We Do In Life and Business*

In life it takes more than just thinking about habits to develop them both for an individual and for an entire enterprise.

Later in the book we will be talking about how to create an enterprising culture but while it's undoubtedly helpful and indeed essential for you as a leader to create and support an infrastructure that enables good habits for a culture to flourish, it also requires each individual to be prepared to take personal responsibility for their own behaviour.

And that starts with you, making a commitment. This will give you the courage to then build your personal capability through conscious thought, planning and application.

Why Do You Develop A Habit?

Think of something that you do habitually. How much effort does it take?

Well, as Charles Duhigg explains in *The Power of Habit,* scientific research has shown that our brains are constantly seeking new ways to minimise effort in order to maximise the energy we can focus on survival. To do this, the brain is always looking to *chunk up* sequences of action into automatic behaviour – a habit – that literally requires no conscious thought; when we're walking or driving, for example.

How Do You Develop A Habit?

All behaviour starts with a trigger that tells the brain to do something and research suggests that a repeated trigger-behaviour pattern starts to forge a neural pathway in the brain – a bit like a motorway - which carries the signals that drive the behaviour. The more often and consistently the brain is triggered, the smoother and clearer the neural pathway becomes – and the more consistent and faster the journey – until at some point automatic, hard-wired behaviour develops a habit. Science has also shown that an action – a trigger-behaviour pattern – has to be repeated every day for between 60 to 70 days for the neural pathway to be well and truly forged.

So, if our brains are actually constructed in a way that make us inescapably creatures of habit, the question has to be *How do we develop habits that bring benefit and how do we change those habits that don't?*

Well, a 2015 MIT[24] study has shown that habit operates in a three-step loop – *Cue-Behaviour-Reward.*

Figure 5.1: Cue - Behaviour - Reward

- First comes *The Cue* – a trigger that tells your brain to go into automatic mode and what to do.
- Next is *The Behaviour* – a physical, mental or emotional behaviour that's triggered by the Cue.
- And then comes *The Reward* – a positive stimulus that tells your brain that the outcome is worth remembering to do again.

The *Reward* stage is especially important because we have to benefit in some way from the *Behaviour* or we won't repeat it – even if in the long term it actually does us no good. In other words, there has to be a pay-off, and the quicker the better.

Take smoking. The *Cue* is that the smoker is stressed, say, or having a cup of coffee or in a social situation. There could be several *Cues*. The *Behaviou*r is smoking a cigarette. And the *Reward* is the stimulus or relaxation that follows, almost at once. There could be health drawbacks in the long-term but in the habitual action there is *Cue, Behaviour and Reward.*

It's like a little story – beginning, middle and end – that's reliable and comforting, because it consistently delivers the expected outcome, the *Reward.*

It's the regular repetition of this story that builds and reinforces the neural pathway that makes a habit so hard to change. As soon as the *Cue* is triggered, we're off down that pathway towards the anticipated end, usually without even consciously thinking about it.

Why Do We Find It Difficult To Create A New Habit?

As we saw in the 4Cs model, creating a new habit and/or breaking an old habit starts with a commitment to change, which can be daunting. Are we prepared to make the effort, to confront difficulties and the possibility of failure?

What's more, when you concentrate consciously on trying to do things differently, the process can often feel really mechanical and artificial and you might question whether the end result will actually be worth the pain of getting there. There is always a phase when the feels unnatural and possibly even slightly fake, at which point you're faced with two choices – to give up or keep practising until it all becomes much more natural.

An interesting way to look at creating a new habit is as a four-stage process of development[25], as outlined below in *Figure 5.2.*

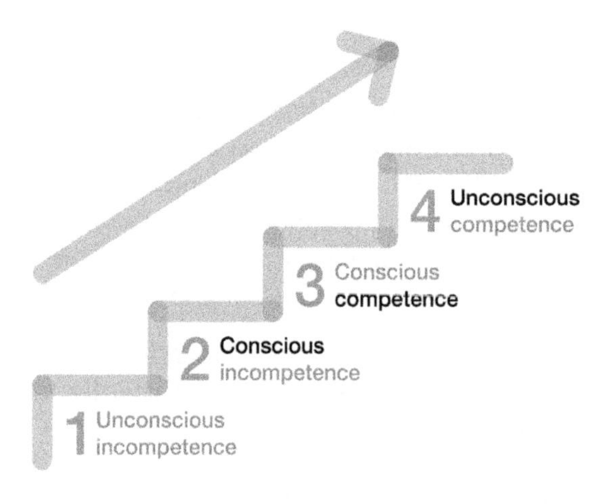

Figure 5.2: Four Stages Of Competence

- *Stage 1 – Unconscious Incompetence* - Everything starts here i.e., you don't know that you lack a particular ability or what it is you're doing wrong.

- *Stage 2 - Conscious Incompetence* - The next stage of change is then to become consciously incompetent i.e. you become aware of what it is you're doing wrong.
- *Stage 3 - Consciously Competence* – The mechanical stage where you're actively trying to change what you do habitually and where it can feel awkward and stiff and mechanical.
- *Stage 4 - Unconsciously Competent* - The final stage where your so practised in your skills that they've become embedded and part of your new habits.

The reason it can be so difficult to change is that when you concentrate consciously on trying to do things differently, it can feel really mechanical and artificial and you can't immediately see the value of committing against the pain it causes you.

There is always a phase when it feels unnatural and you feel slightly fake-ish about it. You are faced with two choices – give up or keep practicing until it all becomes much more natural.

Back to our old friend commitment.

How Can You Create A New Habit?

You can create a new habit by telling a new more powerful story with another, better reward than your current one.

Our smoker, for example, would recognise the *Cue* – a coffee break, maybe – but could tell the story internally, that tobacco smoke actually contains various poisons. So, *Don't have a cigarette!* or *Find a substitute!* – i.e., do a new *Behaviour.* And the Reward could be self- congratulation – *I didn't poison myself* or *I've managed to cut down on my smoking.* Or maybe, *With vaping I get the benefits of the cigarettes and none of the drawbacks.*

In other words, same *Cue*, but different *Behaviour* and different *Reward.* A new story. And of course, the more our smoker reinforces this new story, the more a new neural pathway will be built that eventually makes the old pathway, the old story, redundant. So, the key to changing a habit isn't really will power – it is story power. Committing to a new story and then have the courage to tell and retell it until you have replaced the story of the old habit.

This brings us back to your personal *Purpose, Vision and Values* – which we will look at in more detail in Section 3 of this book. By building them into the *Reward* in every way you can, you consistently tell new stories that drive the creation of new habits that increase your productivity – and of course, the effectiveness of your enterprise.

Cue-Behaviour-Reward. Beginning-Middle-and-End.

Commitment, courage.

Old habit, old story. New habit, new story.

Sounds simple!

How Can Visualisation Help?

If you want to develop a new habit you have to keep repeating it until it is automatic, hard-wired behaviour. The more often you do it, the quicker it will become fixed. It sounds so obvious and easy to do and yet as we all know it can require large amounts of will and self-discipline to succeed.

Amazingly, you can speed up the process by using a performance technique called visualisation.

This involves thinking through every step, every small aspect of the action you are going to take – what it looks like, what it feels like, what it smells like even – in order to reinforce the neural pathway that you are building in your brain. It is like telling yourself a very detailed story about what you are going to do – with a positive, happy ending.

A great example of this process comes from the world champion 110m hurdler, Colin Jackson.

One of the great barriers hurdlers such as Colin Jackson faced was that there was only a limited amount of times they could run the high hurdles at full-pelt in any training session as it was so exhausting. This in turn made it difficult to improve the very precise technique needed to clear every hurdle while sprinting at full speed. To make up for this Jackson would sit down and vividly visualise himself jumping the hurdles and that massively accelerated his ability to improve his hurdle technique.

It must have worked as his world record of 12.91 seconds for the 110m hurdles set when winning the *World Championship* in 1993 stood for over a decade and he remains the 60 metres hurdles world record holder, 25 years after setting his time.

When Is The Best Time To Visualise?

Research has shown that the times when visualisation is most effective are when you first wake up and, best of all, just before you go to sleep. Because when you are in the land of nod all sorts of re-ordering goes on in the unconscious mind and pre-sleep visualisation will give you greater mental clarity the next day.

Exercise

As an exercise, think of one simple thing you would like to do as a new habit and spend five minutes every day – before you go to sleep and/or when you first wake up – visualising it in as much detail as you can. How does it look, feel, smell – and, crucially, what is the *Reward,* the happy, positive outcome at the end of the story?

Use this technique AND take the real action for 21 days – visualisation and action together. At the end of those three weeks, give yourself a mark out of 10 in terms of the positive effect on your behaviour. Then do it for another 21 days, write down your mark again and finally another 21 days. Then review the process and give yourself a final mark out of 10.

Summary

You can't create a culture of effective habits by just talking about it.

The key ingredient to any transformation is your behaviour as the model of everything you want to see happen.

You can invest in huge amounts of money in training and infrastructure, but all this will be wasted if you don't walk the talk.

The good news is that it's perfectly possible to do.

It starts by making a commitment to a new habit and having the courage to address the discomfort this will create.

Understand how habits are created through the three-step loop of your internal story. The *Cue-the Behaviour* and the *Reward.*

Recognise the story behind the habit you want to change and write yourself a new one to guide you as you develop your new capability. It will feel uncomfortable at first but by sticking to things, helped by visualisation at times, you can soon see the benefits.

Part 3
Clarity of Leadership

Part 3
Introduction To Clarity Of Leadership

This part looks at how you can develop *Clarity of Leadership,* founded on our first three principles:

1. A leader's clear personal *purpose, vision and values,* which are congruent with
2. The clear *purpose, vision and values* of their organisation, which are fulfilled through
3. Clarity about what value you're providing for which customer needs.

All of which is held together by a tool called *Strategy on a Page.*

Chapter 6 considers the importance of your personal clarity - your needs and wants and your personal values and how you can incorporate these into your personal purpose and vision.

Chapter 7 presents a tool called *Strategy on a Page (SOAP)* that offers a way to communicate clarity throughout your organisation and effectively delegate responsibility for action.

Chapter 8 shows how to clarify the *purpose, vision and values* of your whole enterprise and ensure that these are congruent with your personal purpose and values.

Chapter 9 covers the importance of clarifying *Market Position.*

A detailed understanding of your customers – not just who they are but also what makes you particularly unique and attractive to them – and where you can find them. Inevitably, you will end up with a number of different combinations, each one of which will need its own unique strategy and therefore its own unique page. We will show how, as these are defined, they you can be used to create a clear picture of your overall strategy and enable you to begin to allocate key areas of responsibility using the *SOAP* tool.

Chapter 6
Principle 1:
Clarity For The Individual Leader

'The organisations we create are a pure reflection of their leaders – their vision, their strengths, their character but also their fears, insecurities, and ego.'

Ben Lane, *Acumen Academy UK*

'Be certain about what you want to do.'

Brendan O' Keefe, CEO *Epic CIC*

Introduction

Why is this our *First Principle?*

Again and again, we find that the stress we observe in leaders on a day-to-day basis originates from their confusion about what they want, not just in terms of what they're looking to achieve but also but how they want to feel along the journey.

Personal clarity is the foundation of any leader's effectiveness. So achieving this is not self-indulgence – it's very practical.

All too often in this sector, leaders' lives can be subsumed by the hard work and battles they face driving the organisation forwards, and important though that dedication and resilience is, ultimately the imbalance that results from making sacrifices elsewhere is bound to take its toll. Nobody wins.

Not only is leaving your real self at the door when you go in each morning stressful and unhealthy, we also have seen again and again how damaging this can be for an organisation and its stakeholders. By contrast, when work chimes with how you want your life to be, you become more productive and everyone gains.

So, in the interests of everyone involved – including you – it's important to get the alignment between the personal and the organisational exactly right. Only by doing this can you maximise the value you're adding to the enterprise. And when everyone can match the organisation's purpose and what they themselves want from the party, work really begins to hum. You have the right people in the right place, committed to a clear set of goals and all supporting each other in making the right decisions to do the right things – for the social enterprise, for one another, and for themselves. It's a win for everyone.

So where do you start?

By clarifying your personal purpose and your personal values.

Personal Purpose

In simple terms, personal purpose is how you want your life to be. You know there are things you love doing and are good at, areas where you can really create value. But is that what you're actually focusing on, where you're currently investing your time and energy? If yes – great. If no – well, how do you feel about that?

What Are Your Needs?

A simple question which, like many things we present in this book, has many answers.

A productive place to start to answer this question is a framework developed by Tony Robbins[26], one of the world's leading thinkers on personal development, who based his framework on the work of renowned psychologist Abraham Maslow and the conflict scholar John Burton.

Maslow famously talked about a hierarchy of human needs, starting with basic elements such as food, water and shelter and working up through safety, love/belonging and esteem to, at the pinnacle, self-actualisation *(See Fig 6.1)*. Burton and others challenged this, however, suggesting that human needs are simultaneous, not hierarchical.

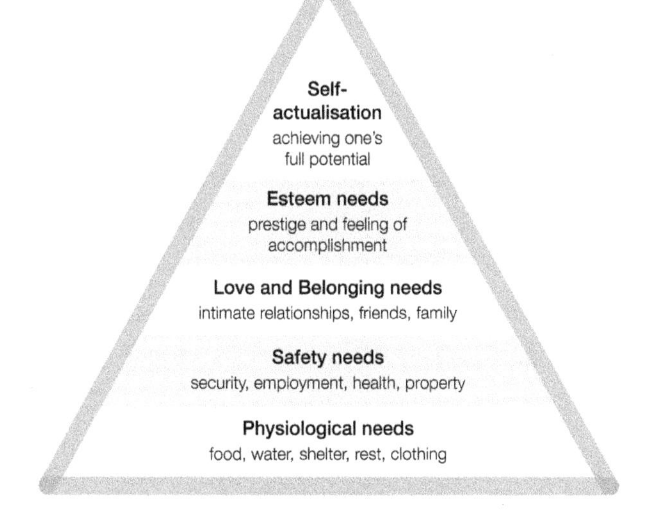

Figure 6.1: Maslow's Hierarchy Of Needs

Robbins synthesised the positions, arguing that everybody is driven by a need to fulfil one or more of six basic human needs. While we all have all six, everyone is unique and so the value we put on each need will differ. Indeed, the emphasis can often shift as we go through life.

1. *Certainty* – that things will unfold as imagined
2. *Uncertainty* – that life will serve up its share of variety
3. *Significance* – the sense of being special or unique
4. *Love and connection* – the feeling of togetherness or intimacy
5. *Growth* – the feeling that we're making progress
6. *Contribution* – the feeling that we're part of something bigger than ourselves

Reflecting on your own current personal mix is a good starting-point for developing a clear personal purpose, so take a little time to complete the following exercise:

Exercise

Reflecting on your life in general (personal and work) write down the answers to these questions:

- Which of the six basic human needs do you habitually meet?
- Which of these needs are not being met currently?
- Which needs would you like to meet more often?
- What are the top three trade-offs or conflicts over what you would like and what you're currently experiencing?

Looking at your answers, how do you feel about what they reveal?

How Can You Turn Clarity Of Needs Into A Clear Personal Purpose?

We have been inspired by our work with Deri Llewellyn-Davies[27], who developed a tool he called *Strategy on a Page (SOAP)* aimed at helping business owners to scale. Deri argues that there are four elements to an individual's personal purpose:

1. Passion
2. Lifestyle
3. Money
4. Exit

What's Your Passion?

What are you passionate about? What is it that you truly love to do? Hopefully, there are things we're all passionate about in our personal lives – but what about life at work? What really floats your boat – and what sinks it?

Passion generates energy and commitment and imagination, while a lack of passion does the exact opposite. Lack of passion means the desire to contribute and create value are effectively locked down – and that goes against the very purpose of having a *4th Sector* enterprise in the first place.

So as a leader you have to be honest and clear about where your passion lies. Or even if you really have it at all where and when it's needed. As Deri notes:

"You have to have passion… That's what gets you through the dark times, that's actually your competitive advantage in a lot of cases... And I mean everybody in the organisation having that passion, there's no excuses for that. And I think that's fudged. I think a lot of people go, *Yeah, oh we love what we do.* Well, really?"

If you're not loving what you do and you've lost your passion, it's either because you built the wrong thing in the first place or you're doing a load of stuff you shouldn't be doing.

What Lifestyle Do You Want?

Big question – what kind of life do you want to live and are you actually living it?

Yes, we all know that work isn't everything – or shouldn't be. But if you have a passion for what you do, plus a strong sense of responsibility – and a lot of people running enterprises do – work can just expand until it seems to take up, well, your every waking moment. That's rarely healthy. External pressure inevitably increases and things can easily start to slide. Everywhere.

So it's in the interests of all busy leaders, the organisations they lead and the customers they serve to get the balance between work, home life, friends and outside interests absolutely right.

You can only do this by being clear about what things are truly important to you. And this means not just talking about them but writing them down.

How Much Money Do You Need?

Money. It can sometimes be seen as a bit of a dirty word in a *4th Sector* enterprise. Not just in terms of what the organisation needs, but also what everyone's paid. Some people seem to think that if you want to do something of social value in the world you should somehow live off fresh air. Which is obviously impossible. You've got to eat, put a roof over your head, support your loved ones and maybe even have a little fun every now and then.

How much money do you need to support the life you want to live? It's a good question, and one that makes a lot of people feel a bit, well, uncomfortable. But it shouldn't, because this is a real need, and failure to address it head-on is only going to mean storing up trouble further down the line.

So, what's your number - in hard cash?

What Is Your Plan For Your Exit?

In the film *Groundhog Day,* weatherman Phil Connors (played by Bill Murray) finds himself destined to live the same day again and again. At first, realising that there are no consequences to his behaviour he thinks it's fun – but his inability to break this repetitive loop soon turns dark. Similarly, it can feel like an endless *Groundhog Day* if you get stuck in an enterprise that you built and are proud of and is doing sterling work – but for one reason or another you feel you can never leave it.

Earlier we introduced the 4Cs framework where we considered our fundamental need to grow and develop and our interviews show how this consistently and strongly manifests itself in the spirit of an entrepreneur.

So, this brings us to a big question many of us tend to avoid – when and how are you going to leave your job? Not necessarily your organisation, just your current job.

Now, some would say it's totally out of order to ask that when you're pouring body and soul into making this thing you're passionate about a roaring success. But they're wrong, because that day will come, even if it's years away. In fact, it's actually very healthy, indeed essential, to start thinking about your exit strategy now. To plan how it will work and what follows on from that. Because you never know what might happen – or when.

This might feel odd right now, especially if you're in the early stages of building something. But if you don't look beyond your current reality you can get trapped – and in the process trap your organisation, too. Too often people are not proactive enough in thinking about succession planning, especially if they've been in a leadership role for a number of years.

So, what is your exit plan?

Personal Values

'Values are like fingerprints. Nobody's are the same, but you leave 'em all over everything you do.'

Elvis Presley (American singer, 1933-77)

Why is it essential to be clear about your personal values?

Why are you leading a *4th Sector* enterprise? Why aren't you running a straight-up commercial venture and trying to make loads of money – or spending your time in a good, solid job?

It's simple. There are things more important to you than just pound signs. Yes, you need to earn enough to live the life you want but what really drives you is your values - what you hold to be important. So you must be able to name them – precisely – for two key reasons.

First, your values will directly impact your behaviour and decision-making, which as a leader will greatly shape your enterprise to be a reflection of you, what you care about and think is important. Being able to name your values will help you achieve clarity and consistency in your planning and decision-making.

Second, one of the greatest causes of conflict and indeed personal stress is when there's a clash between an individual's personal values and the values of the organisation itself. And – depending on the management structure – you might be on either side of that equation.

This makes it essential for you to be clear about your personal values and how they relate to your enterprise. Once you can clearly articulate those values – and the exercise below will help you do that – they'll shine a light on the choices you have to make, at all levels.

Simply, this clarity helps reduce or even remove the stress of decision-making.

If you're starting an organisation, for example, you can consciously use your personal values to help set the organisational values and so ensure that every decision about who you hire - or indeed who you do business with - is considered clearly through this lens.

On the other hand, if you're considering joining an organisation, comparing your personal values to those that the organisation is presenting is an ideal way to know if you're a good fit for each other. If you're not, you have to ask yourself whether you feel in a position to change or influence the organisation – or whether it's simply not the place for you.

These are just two examples. But it's no exaggeration to say that in every work situation being clear about your personal values is a huge advantage.

How Do You Clarify Your Personal Values?

Here are a couple of exercises. Once you've done them you should have a list, ideally of single words, with a short sentence explaining why you feel they're important to you.

You have to be able to articulate and explain them without hesitation, so we recommend no more than five values and fewer if possible. So you might need to prioritise and possibly merge some together into a single, embracing value.

Exercise

Finish this sentence in five different ways – *'I really love it when...'*

And then finish this sentence in five different ways – *'I really hate it when...'*

Now, try to identify the value at the heart of each sentence.

For example, 'I really love it when someone shows a bit of initiative' could mean that you value creativity or risk-taking or courage. There's a range of possibilities.

While *I really hate it when people argue* could mean that you value harmony or collaboration or simply kindness between people. Again, there are different possibilities.

Make a list of all the values you've identified and boil them down to a maximum of five.

How Do You Use Your Personal Values?

The real power of values comes from being conscious about using them consistently. The reality is that whether you're aware of it or not, every decision you make is based on your values. When you aren't clear, however, it can lead to a level of agonising and doubt that too often ends up with the wrong result.

So clarifying and articulating your values out loud, whenever you can, will improve both consistency and impact. Once you stop to consider each and every decision through this same lens and gauge the response, clarity soon follows – about what you want and what everyone else understands you want. Decisions in turn become quicker and easier to make.

Exercise

Over the next few days take your values for a ride.

1. Each time you have to make a decision, consciously view it through the lens of your values.
2. Ask yourself - how does it feel?
3. And can you explain it to anyone else involved? If so, what has been their reaction, not just to the decision but also to how it's been related to a specific value?

Treating every decision in this way will generate learning and increase your clarity and comfort level. It's likely to feel odd at first, as with learning any new habit, but as time goes on you will get more and more comfortable and then only need to consciously reference your values on specific occasions or particularly tricky decisions.

Summary

This chapter has explained how important it is for any leader to be clear about what they want and need.

It has focused on how you can reduce stress by consistently applying this personal clarity in your decision-making process.

We introduced some simple questions to help you reflect on your personal needs – your passion, the lifestyle you want, the amount of income you need to achieve that lifestyle and your strategy to ensure you have a clear plan of how to keep moving forward.

We explained the importance of core personal values, how to go about articulating your own set of at most five core values and how they can be used to understand and then alleviate the many pressures caused when mismatches occur.

Personal clarity, however, is of little value unless it is aligned with organisational clarity, which comes from applying *Purpose, Vision and Values* to your enterprise as whole. But before we look at that we'd like to introduce a tool to help you drive clarity throughout all areas of your enterprise.

Chapter 7
Strategy On A Page – A Helpful Tool For Clarity

Our next two principles cover the importance to *Clarity of Leadership* of combining organisational *purpose, vision and values* with a deep understanding of how your product or service specifically relates to your target customer.

Perhaps the greatest challenge for any leader, however, is how to transmit the clarity that they have to everyone around them. It's how to get everyone facing in the same direction and applying consistent measures of passion and commitment to succeeding in their shared goals. And how to release the full potential of every asset within their organisation in that joint endeavour.

So, at this point we want to introduce a key framework that we've found to be extremely helpful in driving this shared clarity throughout an organisation – *Strategy on a Page.*

What Is Strategy On A Page?

Deri Llewellyn Davis devised *Strategy on a Page (SOAP)* as a simple way for any leader to keep their organisation on track as it grows, no matter what its size, and we worked with him to adapt it specifically for the *4th Sector.*

Deri describes *SOAP* as:

> "An antidote to the traditional business plan that is written and simply sits on a shelf gathering dust. It's a tool for leaders to keep everything simple and in one place – both for themselves and for their whole organisation."

We believe *SOAP* offers an ideal framework to meet the shared challenges referred to above. Not only does it help any leader to decide on the best direction of travel but it also makes it easier to communicate that direction to everyone within their organisation and then fully empower them to achieve success.

Why Is Strategy On A Page Useful?

Keeping the *Purpose, Vision and Values* of our enterprise (the Big Result) at the heart of everything we do is the job of every leader but, as we all know, in the midst of a busy schedule it's not always so simple. It takes discipline, a lot of clear thinking and a lot of clear communication – and this is where *Strategy on a Page* is really useful.

Indeed, whether you're leading an entire organisation or just a project within it, maintaining that lifeline between the *Big Result* and everyone's day-to-day action is perhaps your most important job. And by keeping the *Big Result* front and centre for everyone, *Strategy on a Page* makes this much easier.

It allows any variety of tasks to be both communicated and ultimately delegated within the structure of a page – a distinct and focused set of decisions and actions – without fear of the overall *Purpose, Vision and Values* being diluted or misunderstood. And because the purpose of every task is clear, it empowers everyone, as they can see how their day-to-day activity directly contributes to the *Big Result* you're all working towards.

What Does *Strategy On A Page (SOAP)* Look Like?

Strategy on a Page pulls together in one place all the major elements you need to keep the organisation focused on the *Big Result* you're working for, all the way from the big picture based on *Purpose Vision and Values*, right through to what needs to be done today.

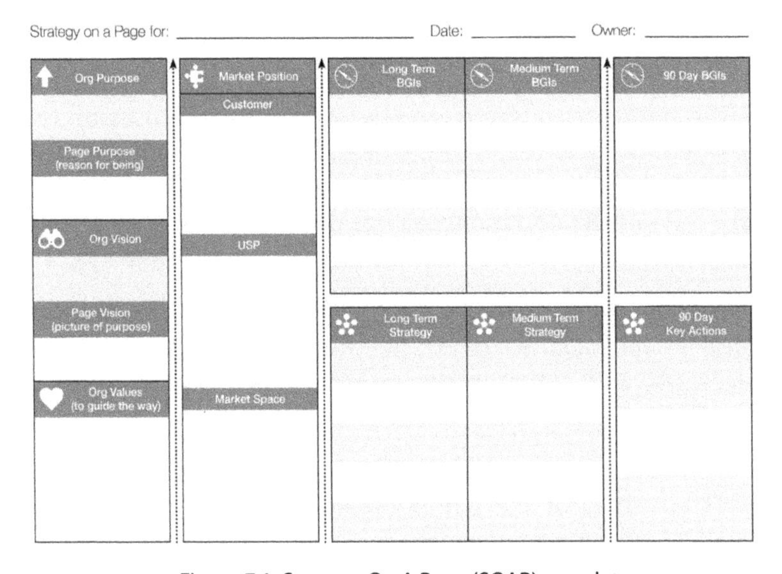

Figure 7.1: Strategy On A Page (SOAP) template

Every enterprise can be broken down into multiple pages, each defined by a unique combination of its key elements. When put together, these pages will in turn provide an instant snapshot of the working whole.

Each page starts with a specific title defining its output and the name of its owner, the person who has been given the responsibility for its execution.

The left-hand side of the page sets out the *Purpose, Vision and Values* of your organisation, to ensure that they can be referenced at all times. This is the *Big Result* for your organisation, which we cover in more detail in Principle 2 in the next chapter.

The left-hand side also includes the *Purpose and Vision* of that specific page to ensure that they're congruent with the overall *Purpose and Vision.*

The next section of the page – the *Market Position* – is the key to deciding the areas of strategy to work on. Each page features a unique combination of one of your *Customer Avatars* (profiles), a *Unique Selling Proposition* that solves a problem for them and a market space where this happens. This works both for internal and external customers and is covered in Principle 3 (Chapter 9).

The third part of the page – two sections – focuses on the execution of the seven key strategy areas (marketing, sales, finance, operations, talent, digital and social value) that make up every project and the measures that will guide everyone on progress. This is covered in Principle 4 (Chapters 10 and 11).

The right-hand side of the page sets out what needs to be done in the next 90 days and the short-term measures of success to guide how you're progressing. This is covered in Principle 5 (Chapter 12).

Taken together, the whole page combines the need for a bird's eye view of the whole organisation with the granular detail of day-to-day planning and action. It ensures that the connection of the execution of the project with the *Big Result* is always visible.

It's a powerful tool.

When Is A New SOAP Page Created?

Every time you introduce a new product or service, or extend an existing product or service to a different location or target customer group, the specific *Market Position* of that new offering will demand an owner and a well-defined strategy, and therefore its own strategy page. Regardless of whether a new page is for a new market, product or internal area of the organisation, it will create another piece to add to a visual representation of your organisation that we call the *Cascade.*

Figure 7.2 below shows an example of how this looks for our company, *Bubble Chamber (2019):*

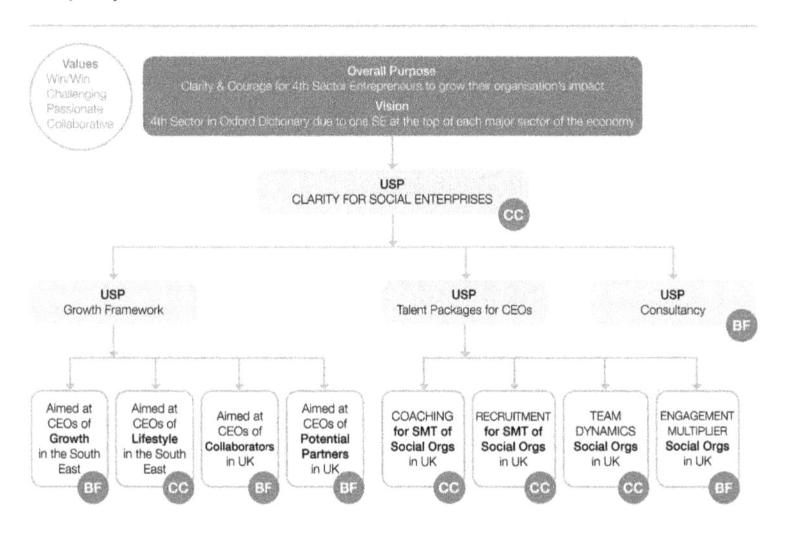

Figure 7.2: Bubble Chamber Cascade Structure For Pages (2019)

Through all of this, your *Purpose, Vision and Values* are consistently there on the left-hand side of every page, core to everything, supporting delegation by giving confidence that they will be applied at every stage and at every level. That's why *SOAP* is such a powerful tool.

Who Owns A SOAP Page?

Given your responsibility for setting your enterprise's overall goals and strategy, the initial structure of your *SOAP* starts with you, as leader, generating the core pages that mirror this strategy.

Fundamentally, though, *SOAP* is a communication and delegation tool that drives ownership and accountability throughout your enterprise. It helps everyone involved in any project understand its direction of travel and how each element of the project fits into successfully fulfilling *The Big Result* – the enterprise's overall *Purpose, Vision and Values*. Once this is clear, responsibility for the page – its ownership – can, of course, be delegated to the right person within the relevant team.

The pages enable individuals at all levels to own areas and issues within their sphere of influence and capability to improve. And, crucially, the pages help everyone see how things are progressing and fitting together.

Where Should SOAP Be Used?

Simple. Everywhere and all the time. The pages offer both a skeleton for your enterprise, a robust framework for thinking and action, and also a kind of nervous system, sending messages to and from the centre and the parts where the action is happening. The pages should be a common language used throughout your organisation – everyone speaks in pages!

So, you might circulate a relevant page ahead of a meeting, say, or mention specific pages during a discussion or in internal communications. In other words, the pages should become reference points that help orientate everyone towards *The Big Result* – your enterprise's *Purpose, Vision and Values.*

Should doesn't mean will, though. *SOAP* can get lost as just another management theory unless it's combined with a single, powerful word – accountability. This demands that everyone's pages are reviewed at regular intervals.

When Do You Review Your SOAP Pages?

We recommend reviews at three intervals.

- Annually as part of long-term planning
- Quarterly as part of short-term planning
- Weekly as a guide to make sure things never go off track.

We'll show in Chapter 15 on *Meetings* how this review process can be easily incorporated into day-to-day activity.

How Does SOAP Drive Empowerment, Accountability And Execution?

SOAP drives empowerment, accountability and execution in three key ways:

- *Clear System Leadership – SOAP* creates a simple, high-level picture for everyone of the inter-relationship of all the different Market Positions of your organisation. You can then share and discuss these with your Board and Senior Leadership to create clear agreement of what needs to be done to direct your organisation.
- *Clear Delegation of Project leadership* – Every *SOAP* page is designated as someone's clear responsibility. At all levels, the pages enable individuals to accept responsibility for areas and issues within their sphere of influence and capability to improve (the rule of thumb suggests a maximum of four or five pages). Crucially this ownership always remains within the context of your organisation's *Purpose, Vision and Values.*
- *Clear organisational language –SOAP* is also a communication tool. It offers a common language throughout the organisation, where everyone can speak pages. It means that you as the leader

can easily talk to any owner of a page within your organisation and be confident that you will both be, well, on the same page! This common understanding also helps everyone involved in a project understand its direction of travel and how this project fits into successfully fulfilling *The Big Result* – your enterprise's overall *Purpose, Vision and Values.*

Summary

This chapter has looked at *Strategy on a Page (SOAP)*, a framework aimed at supporting communication, delegation and accountability throughout an enterprise. It's ideal for reducing the stress that arises from the uncertainty and confusion created by poor strategy implementation.

Within a single page, *SOAP* brings together the *Purpose and Vision* for any specific area of business and *The Big Result* of the whole enterprise, so that whoever owns the page will always keep them compatible.

SOAP helps you break down your organisation into a clear map of its constituent parts and then ensure that the responsibility for each part clearly lies with the right person. And as a leader, it also offers you a way of monitoring and supporting the execution of the individual strategies that need to be implemented to ensure that each of these parts achieves success.

So where do you start to build your *Strategy on a Page?*

The answer's in the next chapter, on our Second Principle, *Clarity of your Big Result* – your enterprise's *Purpose, Vision and Values.*

Chapter 8
Principle 2: Clarity Of The Big Result

*Make sure there is a gap in the market and a margin in the gap. If there isn't it doesn't matter what business you run and how socially valuable you are, you're ***ked.*

John Montague, Director, *Big Issue Invest*

It's all very well to be clear about your own *Purpose and Values* but if these don't match those of your organisation it's pretty much guaranteed that you will be stressed and unhappy. Not only will you struggle to commit fully to leading the success of your enterprise, but it's also highly likely that you will find yourself worn down by continual clashes with individuals both within and outside the organisation over their actions and attitudes.

That's why we've chosen as our second key principle the need for you as a leader to have complete clarity about your enterprise's *Purpose* (its reason for existing), Vision (an agreed picture of where it wants to get to) and Values (how it thinks and acts along the way). As we referred to these three earlier, together they make up your *Big Result* – the main thing your enterprise wants to achieve and how.

Clarity about this is essential not just for you but for everyone involved in the enterprise, from all those on the Board to every member of your front-line staff, no matter how temporary.

So, what does this mean in detail?

PURPOSE

Why Is Defining Organisational Purpose Important?

Every *4th Sector* enterprise is, by definition, driven by a strong social purpose and while yours might seem crystal clear to you it's always possible that it isn't nearly so obvious to others. And if people inside and outside the organisation aren't really clear about exactly why you exist, all kinds of problems can and will arise. Building the right organisation, generating sales, forging engagement internally and externally – all come from a strong, clearly defined sense of purpose, and without one, precious resources can easily be wasted, and opportunities lost. In short, if there isn't complete clarity about your purpose there's every likelihood that you and others could be trying to build the wrong thing.

"Understand what social impact you want to make and don't lose sight of it."

Rose Marley, CEO, *SharpFutures CIC*

Why Is Balancing Organisational Vs Individual Purpose Important?

As a leader there's a very important balance to be struck between the demands of the organisation and your needs as an individual. All too often the lives of *4th Sector* entrepreneurs can be subsumed by the hard work of driving the organisation forwards, and important though that dedication is, ultimately the imbalance is bound to take its toll.

Nobody wins.

So, in the interests of everyone involved, including you, it's important to get the alignment between organisational and personal purpose right.

When your personal purpose – how you want your life to be – is in sync with a clearly defined organisational purpose that everyone understands and buys into, working life becomes a lot more productive and enjoyable.

You don't have to leave part of your real self at the door when you go in to work in the morning.

'Have a really clear organisational purpose that is also true to your personal purpose.'

Tom Kay, Founder, *Finisterre*

'Love your Problem. You need to be more committed to the problem than to any particular solution. This will ensure that the solutions your business provides are robust, and take account of the whole problem, and don't lead to other problems.'

Kresse Wesling, Co-Founder, *Elvis & Kresse*

Where Do You Start In Defining Your Organisational Purpose?

Defining your organisational purpose starts with a simple question – why do you exist? Not you personally but *you* as an organisation, a social enterprise? What service and value do you offer?

Fundamentally, what you offer must solve a problem for people. It must provide a service or a product that meets a need which for some reason isn't being addressed – and by doing so, adds value.

For example, a bus company exists because people can't get easily from A to B – the bus meets their need for transport. It adds value to their lives by solving their travel problem.

So far, so obvious. Except the point can get muddled if you're offering something that you think is great but your potential customers maybe don't – they can't see how it connects to their needs and problems and adds real value to their lives. Suppose the bus company introduces a brand-new bus type, for example. It looks wonderful but is so expensive to operate that they have to reduce the frequency of the service. The company is probably not going to be around for long because it's not meeting its customers' needs.

In short, it's absolutely essential for your enterprise to be able to state, clearly and simply, what its core purpose is – why it exists and the positive difference it makes to people's lives.

So, the place to start when defining organisational purpose goes back to the question – what problem are you solving and for whom?

Can You Live Off A Clear Purpose?

In a word – no.

While it's vital to be clear about the problem your organisation is looking to solve and to match this to your passion as a *4th Sector* entrepreneur, you mustn't forget that a social enterprise is also a business and to succeed it has to make money.

So, once you've defined – clearly and precisely – the value you're creating, you've got to get real and practical about numbers i.e. the size of your market. This means asking who specifically is going to buy what you're offering? How many of those people are out there? And how much money potentially do they have to buy your products or services?

You've got to start asking these hard questions about money and customers – and the answers have to be in numbers. Cash in, cash out, sales, costs. Because only then can you honestly say if you're going to get a return on your – or your backers' – investment. Put bluntly, you've got to ask – is the market opportunity big enough for my enterprise to succeed?

'Invest in articulating your mission clearly so that everyone knows what you are doing and what you aren't doing.'

Sophi Tranchell, Group CEO, *Divine Chocolate*

How Can You Develop Your Organisational Purpose Statement?

Being able to state your organisation's purpose clearly and concisely is a key strength. In a few words you put everyone in the picture – potential customers, suppliers, staff and possible investors. Not only do you and your enterprise come across as focused and on the ball, but stating your organisation's purpose also ensures everyone can sense check it against their own purpose to make sure there is congruence. This can not only help build your confidence but also that of everyone you're dealing with.

So, it's really worth the effort to define your organisation's purpose precisely – in a single sentence. Try the following exercise and see what you come up with. As Deri Llewellyn-Davies says, 'You'll know when you've got it right because when you read your purpose statement there should be little hackles going up on your neck. You should be totally bought into it. It should excite you.'

'Make sure you have a very clear mission ... ours is only eight words.'

Niall McShannon, MD, *CCI Scotland*

Exercise

Write down what you're offering – the problem you're solving and the value you're creating for people – in a maximum of only 10-12 words.

Be ruthless. Cut the fluff. Make every word count. And when you think you're done, try out your sentence on your Senior Leadership Team and your Board (if you have one).

Do they agree? Can they improve it?

Keep at it until those hairs on your neck stand up! Only when it does this are you ready to introduce it to the whole organisation.

Hammering out a purpose statement like this is tough – but essential. At the end of it you'll have a diamond-hard definition of what you're all about that will underpin everything you do. It's the foundation stone. And you'll have the added bonus of getting everyone in your social enterprise onto the same page, too.

VISION

Why Create A Vision?

We all know that people really buy into stories, not numbers.

Once you have a clear *Purpose* the next step is to articulate your *Vision* - a clear picture, visible to all, of what the big result for your enterprise could actually look, feel and even sound like.

The purpose of creating this *Vision* is to inspire everyone – colleagues, customers, suppliers, stakeholders, and potential investors – so they can see the potential that you can see and be motivated to join you in working towards it.

Without a *Vision*, the door is open to all kinds of misunderstandings about where you're headed as an organisation. With one, everyone's crystal clear about where the whole enterprise is going.

Exercise

Do you have a Vision for your enterprise that everyone would recognise and agree on? If you just had one minute in a lift with someone, what's the story you would tell to convince them to follow you?

Take a moment now to write it down, and consider – is it big enough and, most importantly, can everyone who matters see it clearly?

Try it out on your colleagues. Do they find it vivid, inspiring and purposeful?

As with *Purpose and Values* the process starts with you. Fundamentally, the task is to free your imagination to come up with something that everyone can then own and unite behind.

The vividness of your *Vision* comes from feeling deeply what you stand for and seeing clearly who you'll be working with. What type of relationships do you see yourself having with your customers, for example?

The inspiration comes from how your *Vision* makes you feel. Inspiration comes from the Latin *inspiritu*, which means the spirit within. It's something that doesn't require an outside motivational source, that drives you forward, that makes you wake up in the morning and leap out of bed as you can't wait to get to work! And the great thing about this process of defining your *Vision* is you don't need anything to get it started, just pen and paper – and a wide-open mind.

'Pick your partners carefully. One's that share your values, as the wrong type of partners can sink you.'

Sophi Tranchell, Group CEO, *Divine Chocolate*

VALUES

Why Are Clear Organisational Values Important?

Simple answer – they make decision-making so much easier!

Have you ever had the phone ring, look at the screen and whether it's a customer, supplier, colleague or partner had that sinking feeling in your stomach? That's a clash of values!

Organisational values are incredibly useful in helping decide whether a particular customer, partner or supplier is right for your enterprise; who to hire and who to part company with; in helping to identify issues and challenges and then in resolving and overcoming them. As Roy E Disney, long-time senior executive for *The Walt Disney Company,* observed, 'It's not hard to make decisions once you know what your values are.'

Additionally, your organisational values dictate not just how it operates but how it feels and is perceived. Of course, your website, workspace and many other factors are at play, but overwhelmingly it's the everyday behaviour of everyone in your organisation that speaks loudest – and behaviour is always rooted in values. Whether we're open, or not; dedicated, or not – these qualities, positive and negative, are obvious and memorable to everyone.

Values shape your organisation's identity, becoming the core of your brand. They guide decision-making, underpin the way people treat each other, and therefore drive how everyone feels about the enterprise and their part in it. So, agreeing on a clear set of organisational values that match your own and then applying them throughout your organisation is crucial for everyone's well-being – and for their effectiveness.

What Should Organisational Values Look Like?

For values to be alive in an organisation they need to be articulated in a way that's crystal clear, so they can be remembered and acted upon, and so that the inevitable problems that arise when values are forgotten can be avoided.

As with so many things, simplicity is key. We recommend working to arrive at no more than five core values – each articulated by a single word, backed up by a short sentence of explanation. The language should be non-corporate and authentic for your sector. Here are our values at *Bubble Chamber* as an example ...

- *Win/Win* – based on mutual honesty, respect and trust
- *Passionate* – about the 4th sector and the abilities of the people within it
- *Challenging* – in order to maximise potential
- *Collaborative* – as we're more effective together

As an alternative we've also seen organisations that follow a *Rule of Three,* where every value is defined in three beats.

For example, when the award-winning *Haven Holidays* launched a culture change programme in 2011, they defined their values as:

- Yes I Can
- Dare To Care
- Keep It Simple
- Make It Fun
- Do The Right Thing (an exception to the *Rule of Three,* just to keep you on your toes!)

Exercise

Take a moment now to get a sense of the current state of health of your organisational values.

How would your colleagues articulate them? Would they express them in the same way you do? It's well worth the small amount of time and effort it takes to find out.

Try writing them down quickly without looking them up, then ask some colleagues to do the same – and compare notes ...

How Can You Develop Your Organisational Values?

As with *Purpose*, it's essential that as a leader your organisational values are completely aligned with your personal ones. But having clearly defined your personal values, how do you ensure the organisation adopts them?

As a founder, this is easy. You are the first employee and you can ensure that you don't employ anyone who doesn't buy into your values. We explain how to do this in the chapter on *Talent Strategy.*

If you're joining an established organisation, though, things can be more complicated. Its values will already exist, whether or not they're clearly articulated – and its real values might or might not be consistent with the ones stated in the publicity material.

To resolve this challenge, we suggest working to clarify the understanding of each member of your Board and Senior Leadership Team of the organisation's values and to get a consensus of how they are (or can be) applied within the enterprise.

If the organisation doesn't have any agreed organisational values, the best place to start is to share your own and then give both groups – the Board and the Senior Leadership Team – the opportunity to develop them together to the point of unanimous commitment.

How Do You Use The Organisational Purpose, Vision And Values?

Using your organisation's *Purpose, Vision and Values (PVV)* starts and ends with you, as a leader. You need to get into the habit of consciously using them to make decisions - and making sure people are aware of what you're doing.

It's perfectly fine to have the *PVVs* written down on your website or on the wall over your reception desk or in every *Strategy on a Page,* but unless people see them being used consistently by you to make decisions at the very top of the organisation, they will never take them seriously. Which also holds true with your Board and Senior Leadership Team. So you and your senior colleagues must actually know what the organisation's *PVVs* are – and not stumble when asked!

As we talked about in Chapter 3, applying your organisation's *PVV* in this way can feel uncomfortable at first but, with use, your confidence will grow. Spend some time testing how they hold up in real life situations and, as you find yourself and your senior colleagues making better decisions you can start to incorporate the organisation's *PVV* into every aspect of every strategy.

How exactly you do this depends on how big your organisation is, but the aim is to cascade them from the very top right through every single person in your enterprise, so they inform everything you do, individually and collectively. Every one-to-one conversation, every email and every meeting; everyone you hire, how you hire them and how you then develop them throughout their careers – your organisation's *PVV* have to be at the heart of it all.

Summary

In this chapter we've looked at the immense value of having a clear organisational *Purpose, Vision* and set of *Values* – and the importance of ensuring that these are consistent with your own personal *Purpose, Vision and Values.*

We've set out a selection of exercises to help you achieve consensus on your organisation's *PVV* without losing control of the process.

Finally, we emphasised the importance of consistently using the *PVV* to inform every aspect of how your organisation operates.

We now move on to how you ensure your organisation's *PVV* are applied with laser-like focus – in the right place, at the right time, in the right way – to ensure you maximise your opportunities for success.

Chapter 9
Principle 3: Clarity of Market Positioning

'Really understand what you are trying to do...what your product is, why people want it and what makes you unique. Do a proper competitive analysis.'

June O'Sullivan, Chief Executive, *London Early Years Foundation*

Every enterprise has limited resources and it's easy to waste what you have on the wrong things. Arguably, few things are more stressful and frustrating for any leader.

That's why our Third Principle focuses on the need to develop pinpoint clarity in defining the unique solutions your enterprise is offering to a specific set of customer types. It's only when you've nailed down the combinations that are best for you that you're able to decide the best way to achieve success.

We call this process' achieving *Clarity of Market Positioning* – and it all starts with really knowing your customer.

Why Is It Important To Be Clear About Your Customer?

Your social enterprise exists to solve a problem for people. You'll have covered that when defining your *Purpose*. But which people – exactly?

It's important to know, because these people are your potential customers. And the more precise a picture you can build of exactly who it is you're trying to help, the more precisely you can develop strategies to bring your product or service to their attention.

Taking a bus company again as an example, we've established that it exists to solve the problem for people who can't get easily from A to B. But why can't they?

Is it because they don't have a car – and if so, why not? Can't they afford it? Or is there another reason entirely – they're too young to drive, or too old? Or parking in town is such a hassle?

You need to know, as each variation presents the need for you to offer a different solution, a slightly adjusted product or type of service that meets that specific customer's need. And perhaps it has to be communicated in a different way or delivered by a person with a specific set of skills or using specific equipment.

For example, in the case of the bus company, customers commuting to work will require a different approach from customers who might only want to use the service for leisure purposes on a weekend. And some customers are more tech-savvy than others, so this will affect the company's communication strategy.

Without clarity, it's easy for things to get very complicated, for your customers' specific needs to be overlooked, for people in your organisation to lose focus and finally for the solution you offer to be the wrong one.

That's why the first step of being clear of the *Market Position* of your enterprise is to build a precise picture and story of each of the customer types who make up your potential market.

This is often known as creating *Customer Avatars.*

What Is A Customer Avatar?

A *Customer Avatar* is a detailed description of one of your perfect customers (or potential customers) and creating the Avatar starts by articulating the precise problem that you're proposing to solve for this specific person.

Describe their age and gender; where they live and work; how much money they have to spend on solving their problem and what they're going to do with your product and service.

Really drill down and make the picture as vivid as possible. The key is to tell a story about them, as that makes the *Avatar* easier for everyone to remember and talking about them becomes part of the common language of your organisation.

Exercise

Here is a useful set of questions, by no means definitive, to help identify the specific Avatar for each of your products and services – you'll probably have more than one.

1. What precise problems do they have that you can help solve? Think of as many as you can, no matter how small they might be.
2. How old are they?
3. What is their gender?
4. If they work, what type of organisation do they work for?
5. What does their job involve?
6. Where do they get their information?
7. What are they going to do with your product or service?
8. If you're selling to a business, how much do they have to spend?
9. When and how do they decide to spend it?

When you've done that, it can be really useful to give each *Avatar* a name and title. For example, *Bubble Chamber* has one called *Eddie the Confused Entrepreneur.* He's a bit unsure whether his idea is really a *4th Sector* enterprise or a commercial business, whether or not it's financially sustainable and he has other questions, too.

Naming *Eddie* makes him more real, more individual and more memorable, so it's easier to stay focused on him while working out how best to provide solutions to his problems.

What Happens If It's Not Your Customer Avatar Who's Paying You?

What happens if there's someone else stumping up the cash for you to supply the product or service – a government authority, say, or a grant-giving body? Are you working for them or the people with the actual problem?

This is a very common situation in the *4th Sector* enterprise space and it can cause a lot of grief – especially if the demands of those with the money don't seem to match the needs of the people with the problem that you, the *4th Sector* entrepreneur, are there to solve. And the situation can get even more confusing because these two groups can have several different – or sometimes the same – names. The person with the problem can be called:

- the Customer
- the Consumer
- the Client
- the Beneficiary or
- the End-user

And the person with the cash can be called:

- the Funder
- the Donor
- the Contractor (or sub-contractor, if they're part of a longer chain) or
- the Customer (again).

So, who are you working for?

Some would say it's straightforward – *Whoever pays the piper calls the tune.* And that's fine if whoever pays has the same laser-like focus on the needs of the end-user that you have. But what if they don't?

Well, you need to refer back to your *Purpose, Vision, and Values.* What are you trying to achieve, for whom and why? And if satisfying the funder doesn't meet those criteria, why are you taking their money?

So, this isn't just a question of clarity about who you're working for. It's about your integrity as a *4th Sector* enterprise, too. If you compromise that, it's inevitable that things will not end well for anyone.

Why Is Market Position Important?

Having a clear set of *Customer Avatars* is only a first step. The reality is that while all your *Avatars* might all fit under a general problem, each one will have a different specific need to be addressed by its own specific approach. And each approach has its own unique combination of the seven key areas of strategy – marketing, sales, finance, operations, talent, digital and social impact. It can get very confusing.

The solution lies in identifying the *Market Position* of

everything you offer. The clarity this will bring holds the key to building the bridge to the best strategy for everything you do.

'Make sure you have a product that people want. Just because you think it is a good idea doesn't mean someone will buy it.'

Gillian Holdsworth, Founder, *SH24*

How Do You Define Market Position?

You need to answer two key questions for each *Customer Avatar:*

1. What is the *Unique Selling Proposition* - or *USP* - of each individual product or service you offer? What makes it uniquely valuable to each your *Avatars?*
2. How do you define its market space? In other words, who and where – specifically – are your *Avatars* for each product or service?

You have to know.

What Is The USP?

What makes your *4th Sector* enterprise special in solving a problem for your customers?

How does it stand out from the competition? What – in short – is your *USP*, your *Unique Selling Proposition?*

It's a question a lot of people in this sector struggle with, because it's easy to confuse *USP* with purpose or vision – what you're trying to achieve and why.

So, it's crucial to understand why your *USP* is so important and how you can define yours.

Why Is Defining Your USP Important?

If you're selling yourself in the marketplace, one of the first questions your customers are going to ask you is *What makes you different from someone else who also claims to be able to solve my problem?*

If you can't answer that question in a clear, succinct way it will impact negatively on every aspect of your strategy. Without clarity, how can you choose the right people at the right time to do the right job? And how can you develop a clear message for the marketing strategy, which in turn drives your sales and/or funding strategy?

How Do You Define Your USP?

A good place to start to define your *USP* is to find and talk to some real-life examples of the *Avatars* you've created – your customer types – to help you look closely at every element of your product or service, so that you can clarify exactly how it helps to solve their particular problem. By really listening to your customers like this, again and again, so that you truly understand their problem, you can actually create your *USP* with them, hand-in-hand. Investing your time like this can save you from making a common mistake of imposing the answer you think is right – which often ends up as a very expensive error.

So, give yourself the chance to rehearse your ideas in conversations with potential customers and listen very carefully to their response, then refine things in the light of what you learn. Make sure you don't simply hear what you want to hear but that you keep going until your *USP* comes into clear focus.

Why Do You Have To Align Your USP With Your Values?

What happens if your *USP* and your *Values* don't match for some reason – because you develop a blind-spot, say?

Let's suppose, for example, that your *USP* is *Providing out-of-hours support for homeless 16-18 year olds.* It sounds great and is solidly in line with your value of *We care.* But if you can only provide that out-of-hours support by working your staff into the ground, your real value is *We care about our customers – but not about our staff.*

So a mismatch like this between *USP* and *Values* has to be avoided at all costs because it breeds cynicism, lack of trust and, ultimately, the potential failure of your enterprise.

What Is Your Market Space?

Market Space is just that – the space, literal and/or metaphorical, in which you're going to be operating, because that's where your customers are. It actually consists of four spaces.

1. The literal space is the *geography* – the town, city, region, country or continent in which you'll be plying your trade.
2. The metaphorical space includes the *economic sector* in which you'll be working, such as the public or private sector.
3. Plus the specific *activity area* in which you'll be operating – like health or retail or transport (there are many)
4. Plus whether you're going to be working mainly *online* or *offline* – or both.

Taken together with your *Customer Avatars* and your *USPs,* each of those four spaces is going to help you define – and redefine – your strategy. Each variation in your *Market Space* will directly impact the strategy you choose to meet your customer needs.

For example, let's look at *Bubble Chamber's Eddie the Confused Entrepreneur.* He struggles with getting the balance right between making money and making a social impact.

We've defined *Eddie's Market Space* geographically as the UK, economically as the *4th Sector* enterprise sector, his activity area as anything that has a clearly defined social impact, and he operates mainly offline, though we don't exclude online *Eddies.*

On the other hand, we have another *Customer Avatar* called *Sophie* who is *Scared to Scale. Sophie* has a very successful social enterprise aimed at young people but is nervous about how it might be replicated. Her activity area is social and health care, her geographical market space is Greater London and her operation is fully offline.

Each *Avatar* in their *Market Space* needs a different set of strategies. For example, for Sophie we might focus our marketing on specific conferences in Greater London, while we might market to *Eddie* at more general Social Enterprise events.

What Happens If You Have Too Many Combinations?

Combined with your *Customer Avatars* and your *USPs*, each of these four spaces is going to help you define your specific strategies – but beware the danger of drowning in too many variations.

So, there comes a point where you have to prioritise and to do this we recommend a *Rule of Five* – that is, limit each relevant person in your enterprise to no more than five combinations, on the basis that it's really very difficult for any one individual to do justice to more than this without things falling through the cracks.

We'll cover this in more detail in later chapters but for the moment try this exercise.

Exercise

Take some sticky notes and write down as many combinations of *USP*, customer type and market space as you feel are relevant to your enterprise. Don't forget to include products for internal customers as well, such as talent development, IT or finance.

Now choose five that you believe are the most important for your success that you take personal responsibility for.

Then look to allocate the rest to the other people in your organisation, according to their suitability, with no one getting more than five.

Once this is done, lay out each sticky note on a table, with the most important for the income of your enterprise at the top. Once they are all laid out in order you will have created a cascade picture of your enterprise.

What does it tell you?

Market Position 1	Market Position 2	Market Position 3
USP: Business Coaching	USP: Clarity video curriculum	USP: Peer to Peer group
Customer: 4th sector leaders	Customer: 4th sector leaders	Customer: 4th sector leaders
Market Space: SE England	Market Space: Worldwide	Market Space: London

Summary

In this chapter we've considered the importance of clearly defining your customers, really exploring their specific problems and then reviewing the solutions you offer in the light of your assumptions. This detailed consideration means you're likely to end up with a selection of slightly different customer types. To help everyone focus we recommend giving them easy to remember names, backed up by a story that sums up their issues, to create a series of what are called *Customer Avatars.*

Each *Avatar* in turn requires a different the solution, so you then need to look at why the one you offer is uniquely attractive to each customer. This is called your *Unique Selling Proposition (USP).*

Finally, you need to be clear about *where* each *Customer Avatar* exists. This is called defining their *Market Space.*

For example, whether offline or only online will impact on the best way for you to interact with them to solve their problem.

Customer Avatar, USP and *Market Space* together in individual combinations creates a selection of clearly defined *Market Positions,* each of which will point you towards its own set of strategies and therefore require its own *SOAP* page.

Putting all of these pages together cascaded in order of importance to your income enables you to create a simple picture of your enterprise. This in turn completes your first stage of your journey to well-being and effectiveness – *Clarity of Leadership.*

So, now you have a clear picture of where you want to go, what happens next? Well, it's obvious. You need to develop a clear strategy of how you want to get there.

Part 4
Clarity Of Strategy

Part 4:
Introduction To Clarity of Strategy

At this point you'll have clearly defined your *Purpose, Vision and Values (The Big Result),* know your *Customer Avatars* like the back of your hand, and you're crystal clear on the *USP,* your *Market Position* and *Market Space* of every product or service you offer. It's time now to turn all of these into concrete, practical actions in a way that ensures the whole organisation is just as clear as you are.

This is the goal of strategy.

Chapter 10 clarifies the difference between a strategic and a tactical plan, breaking things down into the seven key areas that any *4th Sector* organisation must focus on – *Marketing, Sales, Finance, Social Impact, Operations, Talent and Digital.*

Chapter 11 focuses on our Fourth Principle – that the most important strategy is *Talent.* We define the purpose of *Talent Strategy* as being the recruitment, development and retention of the right people, in the right jobs, at the right time and look at how to achieve this, which includes considering the value of effectively measuring employee engagement. The chapter finishes with a simple exercise, the results of which can often be quite surprising.

Chapter 10
Strategy

'It is important to be strategic. This means you need to invest time outside of your day to day tasks to get stimulation for your thinking from work going on elsewhere, be able to recognise your organisation's strengths and benchmark your activities.'

Lucy Marks, Former CEO, *Compass Wellbeing CIC*

Introduction

As we noted in the introduction to the book, it's easy as a leader to spend all your planning time on short-term tactics, particularly when resources are tight. In this chapter we explain why this is a mistake, both for your personal well-being and the growth potential of your enterprise.

What Is Strategy?

The dictionary definition of strategy is a plan for a major result, the key word being major or, in our terms, *The Big Result*. Deri Llewelyn Davies contrasts this with the definition of tactic, which is a plan for an end result.

Why Is A Strategic Approach Important?

So often in life people are tactical when they think they're being strategic. It's easy to lose sense of *The Big Result* in the face of all the issues we deal with in every area. It's tempting as a leader to focus on tactics – seeking short term solutions – to move things forward. While these are very important, solid strategic thinking is essential to relate these tactics back to *The Big Result* we're looking for.

Strategic thinking will stop you drifting off course and ensure that your ultimate aim – *The Big Result* and specific *Market Positioning* you've defined – are alive and evident in everything you do.

What Are The Key Areas That Make Up A Successful 4th Sector Enterprise Strategy?

There are seven key areas to consider when devising the overall strategy for your enterprise, namely:

- Talent
- Marketing
- Sales
- Finance
- Operations – including product development
- Digital
- Social Impact

Talent Strategy focuses on recruiting, developing and retaining the right people at the right time and in the right place.

Marketing Strategy covers everything you do to bring the value of your product or service to the attention of the people you've identified as potential buyers – your *Customer Avatars.*

Sales Strategy converts the interest of your potential buyers into hard cash i.e. they buy what you're offering.

The *Marketing* and *Sales* strategies have to work together to produce a sales pipeline – a steady flow of customer interest that develops to the point of making a sale (generating £s), and then beyond that to the establishment of a sustained relationship.

Finance Strategy monitors the money flowing in and out of your enterprise and ensures that every penny is used in the right way, at the right time, to maximise your financial health and make sure you're getting the best bang for your buck.

Operations Strategy focuses on how to deliver your product or service to end-users as efficiently and cost-effectively as possible, and how to maintain that efficiency and cost-effectiveness as the organisation grows.

Digital Strategy looks at how the digital technology can be best used to enhance the way that you interact with all your stakeholders. Historically, it's often been included within *Operations* or *Finance* but, on the basis that it impacts on every other strategy, it makes sense to consider it separately.

Social Impact Strategy focuses on ensuring that creating and measuring social impact runs through all the other strategies like a stick of rock, rather than being seen as an add-on.

Who Is Responsible For Creating Your Strategy?

Well, the clue is in the word, because *strategy* derives from the ancient Greek for *general* – *strategos* – which came in time to mean the *general's art* or the *general's plan*. So strategy, by its very nature, is something that's decided at the highest level – which means you, the leader of your organisation.

That doesn't mean that you have to do it all by yourself, of course. While, as CEO, you're obviously central to formulating the strategic design of your enterprise – its *Purpose, Vision and*

Values and its *Market Positions* – when it comes to the detailed strategic planning for the seven key areas it's essential to involve your Board and Senior Leadership Team. In fact, your personal well-being depends on it!

So, you develop the strategy together and then, together, cascade it down throughout the organisation using a frame-work like *Strategy on a Page*. As the leader in this process you have three key functions.

First, is to ensure that any strategic plan fits in with and helps deliver the overall strategic design. Everyone involved has to understand the strategic plan's immediate purpose and how it relates to the bigger picture.

Second, is to see that there is effective working across strategic plans and people don't retreat back into their individual silos. A constant challenge.

Third, is to agree and oversee the measurements of success for the strategic plans that will tell everyone clearly and concisely how they're doing at any chosen point (See Principle 5).

How Do You Check You've Got The Right Strategy?

Before you get cracking on the doing, it can be really helpful to stop and take a reality check – courtesy of a *SWOT analysis.* This is a straightforward and well-known tool that offers a simple way of stress-testing any proposed strategy or plan to consider how it holds up, especially when challenged by things the planners might not have thought about. SWOT stands for:

- Strengths
- Weaknesses
- Opportunities
- Threats

Strengths and *Weaknesses* are internal, organisational aspects of the strategy or plan; while *Opportunities* and *Threats* are external factors that could help or hinder its success.

Typically, the analysis is done simply by dividing a large sheet of paper into four quadrants *(See Fig 10.1)* and then asking for those involved to identify possibilities for each quadrant.

Figure 10.1: SWOT Analysis

So, a *Strength* might be that you've got a great idea, while a *Weakness* is you're strapped for cash. An *Opportunity* could be that there is a clear need for your idea but a *Threat* could be that a local competitor's developing something quite similar.

A SWOT analysis teases out all these different elements. And it's best done with as many of your stakeholders as possible – all together, in groups or singly, it's up to you – because different people will obviously spot different things. And it's essential that everyone speaks their mind honestly and candidly, because the sooner any of the four SWOT elements is identified the better. In fact, it can be just as frustrating to learn further down the line that you've missed a great *Opportunity* as it is for a damaging *Weakness* to rear its head.

Doing a SWOT analysis before you get stuck into the detail of your strategic planning can also help prioritise which of the seven key areas will be the most productive place to start. If *Talent* is a *Strength* but *Finance* is a *Weakness,* start with your finance strategy, and so on.

And, of course, you can use a SWOT analysis to stress-test plans in any area of the organisation at any time.

It's an extremely valuable tool.

What Is The Next Step After You Complete Your Swot Analysis?

After you've completed your SWOT analysis you need to ask a single *Big Question:*

What do we want our stakeholders to be saying, feeling and thinking about us in three years time?

By stakeholders we mean anyone with a significant connection to your enterprise – starting with your customers, then your employees, suppliers, investors (if you have them) and your wider community (however you define it).

The value of asking this question in this way – whether by yourself or, even better, with a group of people to make sure no one gets forgotten – is that it helps you focus outwards on the people you're going to be serving and the value you'll be creating for them, rather than inwards on how your enterprise is organised. Organisation is important, of course, but it can cause us to forget that everything internal ultimately has to serve the external, your enterprise's core *Purpose and Vision.*

How Do You Start To Create A Strategic Vision?

By answering the *Big Question* you start to create a strategic vision of your enterprise's future three years down the line. Think of this as your vision of a key stage on the journey to the *Vivid, Inspiring, Purposeful (VIP) Vision* you created in Principle 2.

Taking a three-year horizon makes it much easier to visualise and quantify something really tangible. But don't be afraid to still think big – in terms of your reputation, if not necessarily your size or revenues.

Strategic Vision

Stakeholders	VISION: In 3 years time... What do we want our stakeholders to say about us?

Stakeholders	VISION: In 2 years time... What do we want our stakeholders to say about us?

Stakeholders	VISION: In 1 years time... What do we want our stakeholders to say about us?

Figure 10.2 Strategic Vision Exercise

Then do the same exercise for two years into the future and then for a year ahead. Thinking like this will really help highlight the gaps between where you are now and where you want to get to.

How Do You Move From A Strategic Vision To Strategic Planning?

The final step is the specific strategic planning to detail the action necessary to bridge the gaps that you've identified and move forward in each of the seven key areas.

Plans for the first twelve months will probably be clearer than for your second and third years, but that's OK – you can adjust as the future unfolds. The important thing is to chart a course in each of the seven key areas, and then set out along it.

What Should Be The Timescale Of The Implementation Of Your Strategy?

One of the key questions you have to ask when you're formulating any strategy is 'How long are we going to give this?' No enterprise can afford to spend limitless amounts of time trying to get things right. So every specific strategy needs a deadline – By the end of *such-and-such a period* we need to see a result.

But what is *such-and-such a period*? A month? Six months? A year? More? The most important thing is to decide on a timescale that drives action, which depends on two key things above all.

1. *Where you are in your development.* A start-up will have a very short cycle, as things can change so quickly. The medium term might be only four to six months, say, and the long term no more than a year. But for a more mature business, a strategy might be set for a lot longer – one to three years, or even more perhaps.
2. *The nature of your enterprise.* Software development tends to have a shorter timescale than social care, for example. Retailing will show results faster than retraining. In short, the timescale of any strategy needs to be bespoke.

Ultimately though it has to be about what makes most sense for you given your understanding at any particular point in your enterprise's development.

Summary

Having clarified *The Big Result* you're looking to achieve and then the *Market Positions* for its delivery, your next job it to put together a clear strategy or a plan to achieve this *Big Result.*

As a leader, you need to be careful not to get sucked into thinking tactically, as this will inevitably lead to your enterprise drifting off course.

To design your strategy, start by considering your organisation's *strengths, weaknesses, opportunities* and *threats* by carrying out a *SWOT analysis.*

Then build a 1-3 year *Strategic Vision* that offers an exciting staging-post for your *Big Vision,* based on the realities of your current circumstances but that still inspires everyone to effective action.

Chapter 11
Principle 4: Talent Is The Most Important Strategy

'Great vision without great people is irrelevant.'

Jim Collins, *Good to Great*

Introduction

Which strategy is the most important for any enterprise? Deri Llewellyn-Davies is unambiguous about the answer. 'The one strategy that rules them all,' he says, 'is talent'.

Why?

Money is great. It buys time, it buys equipment, it buys advertising to drive sales – but while all of these are important, the reality is that if you don't have the right talent, your enterprise will never reach its full potential. *Social Impact* is central to any *4th Sector* enterprise – but if you don't have the people to design the right measures, collect the relevant feedback and respond in the most value-creating way, you'll be lost.

Getting the right people, in the right place, at the right time, is the engine that drives everything.

They give you time – the time to think, to work on the business rather than in it, to focus on what you are good at. And the time to create the balance in your life that's so essential to your personal well-being and effectiveness. They also give you money – through better ideas and better execution. Better ideas not just on how to generate more income but also on how to spend less time and resources doing so.

The right people, in the right place, at the right time will not only have the clearest understanding of the needs of the customer but also of how to meet those needs in the most resource-efficient way.

So how should you go about achieving a successful *Talent* strategy?

As Matt Wilson of *Fuse Events* said in an interview for this book, "Invest in your people."

"Take time to find the right people for your business and, when you have them, pay them as much as you can afford. Train them, engage them in the business so they are valued and give them the opportunity to grow with the business. Your business is useless without your workforce."

What Is The Purpose Of Your Talent Strategy?

In the world of entertainment, the *talent* are the people who appear up on stage. Everyone else in the business works to promote, present and protect those talented, creative people. So, using the word *talent* to describe the people who work in your enterprise might seem a bit of a stretch. But it's not.

That's because, ultimately, however good and useful the idea at the heart of your *Purpose, Vision, Values* might be, it's the qualities – the talents – of the people working with you that determines the outcome. It's the talent that delivers – or not. And because it's so vital to your success, it's essential to have a well thought through talent strategy – an overall plan for the recruitment, development and retention of the right people, in the right jobs, at the right time – so that your organisation can deliver the very best results for your customers.

Exercise

Consider your current *Talent* strategy and give yourself a mark out of 10 for how well you feel it deals with the recruitment, development and retention of *Talent* for your enterprise.

Now consider two things you could do in each of those three areas that might increase that mark by 2.

'Surround yourself with the right people.'

Gina Rowlands, Managing Director, *Bevan Healthcare*

Who Is Responsible For Your Talent Strategy?

Who is responsible for your organisation's *Talent* strategy, for measuring, developing and delivering it? Well, it shouldn't really come as a surprise by now to hear that buck stops with you – the boss, the CEO. Which means that it starts with you, too. Because it's you who has to stand behind it one hundred per cent, to drive it on and see it that it's delivered.

That doesn't mean you have to micromanage the strategy, of course. You couldn't afford the time even if you wanted to. Rather, you need to invest your time in the people – the talent – who are going to help you to do all the things that need to be done. So, who are these people exactly?

According to Caroline Ward, the former Head of Talent at *IMG,* the global sports event and talent management company, 'It might be HR people or an HR service. But probably more importantly for most organisations certainly small organisations, it's your own managers, it's your own hierarchy, however big or small that is.'

In other words, your *Talent* strategy is really something that everybody needs to own and take part in. It's shared throughout the organisation, so that every manager and every supervisor knows what they have to do in order to fulfil their part of the responsibility to deliver it.

'You have to have good people all around you at every level. Every relationship is built on trust – and trust is our biggest asset.'

Dai Powell, Group Chief Executive, *HCT Group*

Who Is Your Most Important Hire?

Behind almost every successful leader, in any field, is a key person they're reliant on to get stuff done. The examples are legion.

In the tech world, for instance, they're sometimes known as the adult in the room; people such as Sheryl Sandberg supporting Mark Zuckerberg at *Facebook*, Eric Schmidt supporting Larry Page and Sergey Brin at *Google*.

Their chief characteristic is that they're hard-nosed, pragmatic doers.

In their book *Rocket Fuel*, Gino Wickman and Mark C Winters, founders of *EOS*[28] - *Entrepreneurs Operating System Inc* - describe the ultimate dynamic duo for an entrepreneurial organisation as the pairing of the *Visionary* and *Integrator.*

The *Visionary* is the person who had the original idea, perhaps created the company, and is driven by the need to expand and grow. They tend to have lots of big ideas, enjoy creative problem-solving and they revel in big relationships and selling. Unfortunately, they can also have limited patience, be distracted by the latest *Big Thing* and be a constant source of disruption.

By contrast, the *Integrator*™ (often called the General Manager, Chief Operating Officer or Chief of Staff) thrives on putting systems and processes in place to get things done.

The Integrator™:

- possesses the ability to create harmony amongst the major functions of the business
- ensures effective communication throughout the organisation
- holds people accountable and achieves consistency of execution
- resolves issues effectively, solving problems in a practical, fair manner
- demonstrates a relentless obsession with values alignment and clarity of purpose
- understands the Visionary and helps them transform their ideas into functional plans for the company.

In simple terms the Integrator provides the glue that holds together the people, processes, systems, priorities and strategy of the company.

A number of leaders, often through experience, are able to develop the knowledge and indeed the skills to be both the *Visionary* and the *Integrator*™. But the reality is that when they take on both roles they tend to fail at both, as they have to work so hard at the role that brings them little joy and doesn't play to their inherent strengths, which they tend to take for granted.

Given that so many *4th Sector* enterprises are started by an individual with a vision of a big idea, it's almost certain that the most important hire for your success – and your personal well-being – will be your *Integrator*™.

How Do You Develop A Successful Talent Strategy?

To develop a successful Talent strategy you need to take the following steps:

1. Work closely with your Integrator (if they're in place).
2. Create a picture of your organisation, using *SOAP*, broken down in separate pages.
3. Draw a *Talent Tree* (see below) showing the business as it is now and the key areas of responsibility.
4. Map your current employees onto that *Talent Tree.*
5. Draw a *Talent Tree* for twelve months in the future.
6. Create a strategy to address the gaps that will appear through the development, removal or recruitment of people.

'Invest proper time and care in recruitment. You can never be too thorough ... we sometimes underestimate how much care is needed.'

Lea Esterhuizen Founder *&Wilder*

Step 1 – Work With Your Integrator™

Entrepreneurial leaders are often crystal clear about the importance of their people but struggle with the nuts-and-bolts detail of the things that really make the boat go faster. That's why we recommend as a first step to get yourself a partner in crime; someone who'll make sure that things will get done.

If you're lucky you'll already have someone in place but if you haven't then get do whatever you can to get a good *Integrator™*. If you can't afford someone full-time, then scrape the bottom of the piggy bank and get the money together to hire someone part-time. You'll make a multiple of that investment before you know it, simply from doing better things in less time.

Once it's set up properly - and there might be some friction at the beginning, as the roles are defined – your job in the partnership then becomes that of an enabler rather than a doer. You determine the big stuff like *Purpose, Vision and Values,* the job profile and compensation; you can be involved in the interview process if you want but otherwise you are free to get on with your job of leading the organisation. The rest you leave to your *Integrator.*

'Work out your weaknesses.
Then find the people to fill those gaps.'

Kresse Wesling, Co-Founder *Elvis & Kresse*

Step 2- Draw Up An Overall Picture Of The Key SOAP Pages Of Your Organisation

Once your Integrator is in place, the next step involves reviewing the *Cascade* of all the *SOAP* pages that you've created by following our Second Principle (see Chapter 8).

The purpose shown on every page will help define the job of the person who owns it, their responsibilities and areas of accountability. This in turn will provide an indication of the attitudes, knowledge and skills required for the successful delivery of that page.

By repeating this process you'll be able to map out all activities within your organisation as it currently stands, see how they relate to each other, consider how the responsibilities and accountabilities flow – and maybe identify some gaps.

'Treat your staff well, make pay fair, especially for those at the bottom end of the pay scales: it's unjust to pay people below the living wage just because it's the market rate. The benefits from paying well – in terms of increased staff commitment, lack of stress about debt, and improved retention – are huge and often underestimated.'

Andrew Preston, Founder, *Exchange Supplies*

Step 3 – Draw A Talent Tree Of Responsibilities

Once you have your list with their respective pages, take a pad of sticky notes and write a single job/role on individual notes. Against each job write down its overall purpose, the role that the job fulfils within your organisation and the pages that job owns.

For example, a sticky note for the job of Office Manager could define their overall purpose as *To see the office runs smoothly for all staff.* Achieving that purpose might then include products such as *providing IT service for all staff, maintaining a clean work space and ensuring the use of utilities are optimised.*

To take another example, a sticky note for the job of Head of Accounts might define their purpose as *To ensure accounting is compliant and up-to-date for the Finance Director* (and not just *To do the monthly accounts).* Their outputs could include *producing a monthly profit and loss account, producing a quarterly cash-flow projection* and *paying all creditors on-time.*

Once the overall purpose and output for each job are defined, you can start to break down the job roles, taking accounting again as an example of this might feature tasks such as to be responsible for:

- Updating the cashflow weekly
- Keeping the invoices up to date
- Ensuring that telephone calls are answered promptly

Finally, you need to break down the key areas of knowledge, key skills and – crucially – the values and attitudes that are demanded in that job.

'Make sure you have the right team in place, who are flexible and committed.'

Gillian Holdsworth, Founder, *SH:24*

Step 4 – Map Current Employees Against The Talent Tree

The next step is to review the people you currently have in those roles and see whether or not there's a good fit between the individual and what they're doing – or supposed to be doing.

At this point you should be able to put everyone into one of the following three categories:

1. Right person, right job
2. Right person, wrong job
3. Wrong person, wrong job

This simple but effective filter will also give you an idea of real or potential pressure points, where either someone has more responsibilities that they can reasonably handle or where there are responsibilities but no capable people to take them on.

'Identify and surround yourself with champions who believe in the business and share your vision. Ruthlessly shred the professional saboteurs that you have inherited.'

Neil Woodbridge, CEO, *Thurrock Lifestyle Solutions CIC*

How Can You Take The Emotion Out Of Assessing If Someone Is A Good Fit?

Dealing with the *Talent* in your organisation means dealing with human beings, individuals, all of whom will have some kind of relationship with you. Some you'll like, some not; some you'll feel responsible for, others less so. But towards everyone you'll have feelings of some sort that could affect your ability to make the right decisions for your enterprise. So, to ensure you make the right calls we suggest you invest in 'Understanding First'. *(See Chapter 14 for some tips.)*

This means making sure that you're clear about the personal *Purpose and Values* of every employee. The ideal is that these align with those of your organisation, just as yours do, because sometimes the smallest misalignment can cause problems.

It might therefore be worthwhile at this point to invest in a profiling tool, as these can be helpful in highlighting things such as a preferred approach to work that won't necessarily be clear from simple observation. For example, here's a great tool developed by Wickman and Winters at *EOS - Entrepreneurs Operating System*, which we have adapted and call the *Talent Matrix.*

Talent Matrix

Employee	Win/Win	Challenge	Passionate	Collaborative	Knowledge	Skills	Cut-off
Lucy	3	3	3	3	2	2	
Joe	3	3	3	3	3	3	
Ida	2	1	2	2	2	2	
Fred	1	2	2	1	3	3	

Figure 11.1: Talent Matrix

Along the top you write your organisational *Values* (each in their own individual column. In this example we have used *Bubble Chamber's*) knowledge and skills.

With the understanding you have gained of each employee, give them a mark of 3 if they consistently meet the criteria that defines each of these columns within the context of your enterprise , 2 if you're unsure and 1 if they don't. And set an overall *Cut-off total.*

When you've completed the matrix for each member of staff you should end up with a clear indication of those who are well above your *Cut-off point* – the right people in the right job; those who are well below it – the wrong people in the wrong job; and those who are in and around the *Cut-off point* – possibly the right people in the wrong job.

'Hire for attitude first and then aptitude. You can achieve almost anything with a motivated and committed team who are aligned around positive goals.'

Kresse Wesling, Co-Founder, *Elvis & Kresse*

Step 5 – Draw A Talent Tree In 12 Months

When you've drawn your *Talent Tree* it's useful to draw a second tree, this time predicting the Talent you're going to need twelve months from now to achieve your strategy.

Comparing the two will quickly identify any future potential gaps, person by person and job by job.

Step 6 – Create A Talent Strategy To Move Forward

At this point you should have significant clarity about:

- the people you feel have the right attitudes and capabilities to develop;
- those who don't;
- and the gaps you have to fulfil through recruitment.

As long as you're structured and disciplined, it should be pretty straightforward to draw up a Talent Strategy that sets out how you will address each category and then decide what measures will tell you how successful you are in fulfilling them.

'If you can't measure it you can't improve it.'

Peter Drucker[29]

Why Is Measuring Employee Engagement Key To A Successful Talent Strategy?

87% of workers around the world are not engaged in their jobs. (Gallup, State of Global Workplace 2014)

For many organisations *Talent* is often far and away their biggest overhead, yet it's common to find no agreed measure of what amounts to success when it comes to implementing a *Talent* strategy. Rough measures such as wages/salaries as a percentage of turnover and overall staff turnover are useful but can also be misleading without the proper context.

Investing in a robust process of measuring what is commonly called *employee engagement* provides that context. Poor levels of employee engagement can manifest itself in a variety of ways – high sickness and absenteeism rates, accidents, stealing and overall poor quality of outputs – that can all too easily get hidden within a set of financial figures.

An effective measure of employee engagement provides a leader with a compass to lead and develop talent strategy. Done well, this not only offers an early warning of potential problems; it also offers the opportunity to collect and build on and maximise the value from the collective intelligence of the whole organisation.

What Is Employee Engagement?

Measuring employee engagement is a way to understand and describe, both qualitatively and quantitatively, the nature of the relationship between an organisation and its employees.

Are employees fulfilled by their work? Do they support the *Purpose, Vision and Values* of their organisation? Or are they doing the bare minimum – or even actively damaging its output and reputation?

What Drives Employee Engagement?

'The single most important driver of engagement is the extent to which people believe that senior management has a sincere interest in their well-being.'

Towers Watson, leading Global HR consulting company

When broken down, the 'sincere interest' identified in this statement is made up of six key elements:

- *Clarity of job profile* – How clear is the employee about what they're expected to do in their job? How able do they feel to deal with the barriers that get in their way?
- *Clarity of improvement opportunities* – How clear is the path to improvement?
- *Congruence of Purpose and Values* – How clear are the company's *Purpose and Values?* Does the organisation *walk the talk*? How do the company's *Purpose and Values* match the *Purpose and Values* of the employee?
- *Clarity of internal communications* – Does the employee know *what is going on* when they need to?
- *Relationship with their boss* – How does the employee they feel about their direct boss/line manager? A poor relationship is almost guaranteed to lead to disengagement.
- *Quality of feedback loop* – Does the employee feel understood? How do they feel about what actions arise from that understanding and when they arise? How supported do they feel?

Simply put, the greater the number of these questions that can be answered positively, the more the employee will be engaged with and committed to the organisation.

What Are The Key Barriers To Effective Employee Engagement?

The barriers to effective employee engagement fall into two distinct but related categories – accurately gathering information on the current reality and then implementing any needed changes.

- *The time it takes to design, collect and report on the current situation* – the process can be very resource-intensive in terms of time or money or both.
- *The actual process of gathering information* – the process for employees to give their feedback needs to be easy and straightforward.
- *Poor response to the feedback* – if you aren't seen to act on the feedback you get through the process of gathering information you will definitely lose any of the goodwill you've gained from asking for it in the first place.
- *An inconsistent measure of success – soft* feedback about feelings and attitudes is important and useful, but any process aimed at improving things needs a consistent, quantitative way of collecting feedback and measuring progress; in other words, it needs numbers.

What Are Some Tips For Running An Effective Employee Engagement Survey?

Here are five things to bear in mind when planning an effective employee engagement survey.

- *Create an ongoing dialogue, not an event* – Annual surveys produce a long list of issues that take time to sift and prioritise and it simply isn't possible to address them all. By carrying out the survey quarterly it's possible to create more of a dialogue that helps to manage expectations by addressing a few things at a time.
- *Use the same questions and process* – This gives you a clear way of measuring progress. Gallup's Q12 survey[30] covers the key areas and offers a good place to start.
- *Make it anonymous* – It can take time to win the trust of employees, so making the responses anonymous (or indeed, if possible, the entire dialogue) will lead to a more effective process.
- *Make it easy to complete* – The survey should be something that people can do in 10-15 minutes.
- *Make it easy to report and respond* – You need to design a process that doesn't require hours of reporting and collating, so you can give a quick and clear response.

But What If We Can't Afford It?

Yes, running an effective employee engagement survey takes time and money – but can you afford *not* to do it?

Almost every *4th Sector* entrepreneur we come across has made at least one terrible *Talent* decision in their career, yet it's rare for anyone to say how much it's actually cost them.

Usually it's just accepted as a cost of doing business, without calculating a clear number of the wasted salary, time and opportunity cost.

In truth, though, the same could be said about pretty much everyone who has ever hired anyone. In fact, *Harvard Business School* points out that 80% of employee turnover is the result of bad hiring decisions[31]. Despite this, *The Chartered Institute of Personnel and Development* notes that when measuring overall labour turnover rates and the associated cost *'just 15% of organisations in the UK reported that they calculate the cost of labour turnover.'*[32]

What Are The Costs Of Poor Talent Decisions?

So how much does a poor *Talent* decision cost?

In a detailed 2014 study[33] across five key sectors (IT/tech, accounting, legal, media/advertising and retail), *Oxford Economics* calculated that the loss of an employee earning an annual salary of £25,000 has an average financial impact of £30,614, ranging from £20,113 for retailers to £39,887 for legal firms. These costs take into account the impact of lost output while a replacement gets up to optimal productivity, as well as the impact of recruiting and absorbing a new worker.

More recently, the *Recruitment and Employment Federation (REC)* and leading UK job search engine Indeed, published a study[34] in which they calculated that a poor hire at a middle management level salary of £43,000 could end up costing a business as much as £132,015.

How Do These Costs Breakdown?

Many of these costs are easy to calculate while others, while no less impactful, require more consideration. Direct costs such as recruitment fees, wasted salaries, direct training and compensation are obvious. A bad hire, however, can also have an adverse impact on staff morale, productivity and the reputation of the business.

In *Figure 11.2* we can see how the REC report broke it down:

REC Report Table

Factors to Consider	Details	Cost Calculation	Cost to You
Wasted salary	Time the person has been with you	% of average annual earnings	
Increased sickness/ absence	Over the average	% of average annual earnings	
Professional fees	Both in terms of the settlement and potentially crisis management	- Lawyers' fees - Cost of employment tribunal	
Compensation/ salary settlement	This cost is higher the more senior the position	£ agreed	
Training	Wasted	Specific to the person or share of annual cost	
Replacement cost	Internal time and external costs spent on new recruitment process as well as new training Reduced productivity until new recruit reaches optimal productivity (average 28 weeks)	- Advertising costs - Agency fees - % of annual earnings of hiring managers and interviewers - Induction and training costs - % of annual earnings of new recruit - Cost of any interim staff - Cost of co-workers and supervisors while they get up to speed	
Cost of business	Costs associated with missed opportunities, not just while working but until the new hire is up to speed	Calculate the total revenue by the number of employees and then the number of weeks	
Fraud	Theft, embezzlement and other fraudulent activities	- Financial loss - Legal fees - Damaged reputation	
Impact on staff morale	From seeing how a colleague behaves and is treated	- Lost productivity - Increased staff turnover	
Impact on reputation and brand	That affects both existing and prospective clients	- Time spent managing this - Professional fees getting help	

Figure 11.2 REC Report Table

Take as an example, an enterprise with 30 employees that decides it wants to develop an area of its business to generate an additional £150,000 of turnover, with a net profit of £10,000 in the first year.

- It looks to hire a person at a salary of £32,000 (plus NI) to lead the project and promotes one person internally to support them for a salary of £25,000 (plus NI).
- It advertises online for both positions (the new one and the one that has opened up due to the promotion) using a standard job description and receives twenty applicants for each job and decides to interview four for each position. They have a second interview for a shortlist of two before offering the two positions.
- Two desks are allocated in their office for the two new positions and computers are purchased.
- Both people have a one-week induction under the supervision of the COO.
- The project leader's job is reviewed after one month & three months by the COO. The promoted member of staff resigns after four months. The COO voices concerns with the CEO after three months, so the six-month review involves the CEO after which the project leader is given a month's notice for non-performance.
- The decision is taken to cancel the project.

So what did it all cost? In total, almost £56,000 – if not more.

- Wasted Salary – 7 months plus 4 months of support staff - £30,000
- Wasted Management Time - £2,500
- Wasted Office Space - £3,700
- Wasted Coaching - £3,000
- Cost of hiring - £1,500
- Loss of business – £15,000
- Impact on staff morale, reputation – more than you want!

Summary

The most important strategy is *Talent* strategy – your plan to recruit, retain and develop the right people, in the right place, at the right time to achieve your *Big Result.*

Within this, your most important hire is your Number 2, your deputy. As the leader you're responsible for the *Big Result* but as soon as possibly can you need someone to free you up from working in the business so that you can work on it. You need someone you can trust to get stuff done.

All strategies need a way of measuring progress and for *Talent* it is centred on employee engagement.

An effective *Talent Strategy* costs time and money but do the following exercise and ask yourself – can you afford not to make that investment?

Exercise

Think of an occasion when you have ended up with the wrong person, in the wrong place, at the wrong time and allocate a cost under as many of the headings set out in *Figure 11.2* as you think are relevant.

How do you feel about that figure?

Then calculate your staff turnover last year – the number of people who left and joined – and multiply 80% of this figure by your average staff salary based on the *Harvard* figure for bad hires.

How do you feel about that figure?

'Focus on your team to build one that has diversity in both skills and mindsets.'

Jack Farmer, Co-Founder, *LettUs Grow*

Part 5
Clarity of Culture

Part 5
Introduction To Clarity of Culture

Many social entrepreneurs we meet have worked through their *Clarity of Leadership* and have a clear strategy to achieve what they want but still end up frustrated at getting people to follow through and take responsibility to get things done.

In short, they're frustrated by the culture of their organisation.

What Do People Mean When They Talk About Culture?

In its simplest sense, culture is how people behave in different groups and environments. The culture of a football match is different from the culture of a religious ceremony is different from the culture of a large corporation, even if exactly the same people are involved. And within those different cultures there are also many variations, of course.

In short, culture might be defined as *The way we do things around here*. But what are the core ingredients, the key elements that create culture? And how can you adjust the mix to create a culture for your enterprise that really flies?

What Makes An Enterprising Culture?

The key to creating an enterprising culture lies in a single word – unity. And that comes about through striving for:

- Shared *Purpose, Vision and Values*
- Shared *Strategy* or plan of action
- Shared habits of behaviour – the way that people within your organisation consistently respond and act in certain situations

We've looked in detail at the crucial importance of *Clarity of Leadership* and *Clarity of Strategy* but in our experience without certain clear, shared habits of behaviours it's common to see organisations really struggle – or even fall apart.

So, What Exactly Are We Talking About?

We believe these shared habits are embraced by our last three key Principles.

- Chapter 12 - *Clear habits of Measuring Success*
  Understanding what information you need to collect and analyse consistently, over time, to help guide your enterprise to success.
- Chapter 13 - *Clear habits of Accountability for Execution*
  Creating a culture of accountability that ensures things get done in a timely and efficient way.
- Chapter 14 - *Clear habits of Communication*
  Establishing a communication culture that maximises mutual understanding and creativity and minimises the waste of human energy and resources.

Culture, above all, is about how individuals interact with each other and so our last chapter in this part looks at everyone's favourite regular activity – meetings.

Chapter 12
Principle 5: Clarity of Measurement

'What we measure affects what we do and if our measurements are flawed, decisions may be distorted.'

Joseph Stiglitz, Amartya Sen and Jean-Paul Fitoussi
Mismeasuring Our Lives (2010)

Why Is Clarity Of Measurement Important In Developing An Enterprising Culture?

Without measurement we're lost. We don't know where we're going, how we're doing along the way and, above all, whether we've actually arrived. Clear, effective measures shape the way we all think, learn and interact and are fundamental to a sane culture within any social enterprise. Without them it's impossible to execute, delegate and communicate effectively.

It's simple. If you want to grow your social impact, you need to board the train of measurement, full-steam ahead.

But how…?

What Should You Be Measuring?

Basically, you need to measure the things that tell you how effective you're being in serving your purpose. Deri Llewellyn -Davis suggests that a leader calls these their *Business Growth Indicators - BGIs.*

Imagine you're driving a bus. Your purpose might be to transport our passengers safely from A to B in a way that delights them. They're your customers and they'll probably define delight through some combination of time travelled and comfort.

On that basis, what's the key information you need to be sure that you're fulfilling your purpose during a journey?

For time travelled – your speed, the traffic and the route conditions. For comfort – the temperature in the bus and maybe a simple measure of customer satisfaction. There might be other information but these indicators are vital. And, crucially, you need to know them at a glance because if you can't see right away that you're, say, driving too fast – well, you can imagine the outcome.

BGIs are like an instrument panel for your enterprise. They're a set of half-a-dozen or so key numbers that will tell you – at a glance – how well your organisation is doing. Whether it's growing or contracting or just ticking over. In the world of accountability, everyone responsible needs to know the key *BGIs* for the organisation and how these relate to the key numbers for their *SOAP* pages.

Exercise

Write down the five or six key *Business Growth Indicators* that you currently use to tell you how your enterprise is doing as it fulfils its purpose.

Why Do We Emphasise BGIs And Not KPIs?

Key Performance Indicators (KPIs) are important as they focus on how parts of the system are operating but, crucially, they're not a measure for the system overall. And having clarity of that bigger picture is essential for your effectiveness and personal well-being.

That doesn't mean that *KPIs* aren't useful. The people responsible for a specific area of the business will likely use a selection of KPIs to guide them on how they're doing in working towards perhaps one or two of the *BGIs* that are relevant to their specific *SOAP* pages.

With your bus, for example, you'll have a mechanic who's responsible for all the moving parts. The *BGI* relevant to this might be the number of hours the bus is off the road being maintained. But the mechanic might also have KPIs relating to the efficiency of the engine and the level of fuel required to maximise this efficiency.

The Depot Controller, on the other hand, is responsible for your timetable where their *BGIs* will be the frequency of buses leaving the depot, while their KPIs might relate to the drivers' rotas, the time taken to clean the buses and their arrival time at each destination.

Who Decides On The BGIs?

There's a simple answer to who decides on what the *BGIs* should be – and one that's a bit more complicated.

The simple answer is that *BGIs* are such key numbers that only you, the leader, can make the ultimate decision. Only you can decide what to measure that's relevant to the success of your social enterprise. And it follows from this that – ultimately – the *BGIs* are for you. They let you see the big picture of how things are going because that's your responsibility.

The more complicated answer is that, although you're the boss, you're not the expert on everything – though you probably already know that. So, you need informed and experienced input to help you decide on the relevant *BGIs*. And, once again, this includes people both inside and outside your enterprise.

Inside starts with your Board and those you hold responsible for the SOAP pages that set out the design and implementation of your strategic planning – in marketing, sales, finance, impact, digital, operations and talent.

Outside means suppliers and possibly specialists of one sort or another. But most of all, it means your customers, because why measure something that doesn't in the end affect their experience of your product or service?

What's the point?

Put together, wide-ranging input like this will ensure that the *BGIs* you choose are not just relevant – they're actually owned and understood by the very customer-facing people who collect the data. It follows from this that – ultimately – the *BGIs* can't be for your eyes only. Who knows what other people might spot that you don't and what happens if you're out of action for some reason?

To sum up then, you, the boss, have the ultimate say on your organisation's *BGIs.* They're the stars by which you personally steer the ship. But as many relevant people as possible should contribute to their formulation, so that they're used throughout your enterprise to inform all decision-making, especially decisions that directly respond to your customers.

'Don't abdicate your financial stuff ... it is not good enough to say you are no good at finance.'

Susan Aktemel, Founder, *Homes For Good*

When Do You Use Your BGIs?

Asking when to use your *BGIs* is a bit like asking, *When should a pilot look at the plane's instruments?* The answer, obviously, is he or she should keep an eye on them the whole time – it's a key part of the skill of flying. But there are times when the instruments need particular attention – during take-off and landing, for example.

Your *BGIs* are like this. They're indicators, signs of how your enterprise is operating at that particular checking-point. *Keep an eye on* mode is basically continual and reactive, while *particular attention* mode is more planned and deliberate.

In *keep an eye on* mode, *BGIs* are useful for flashing an early warning that things might not be going as planned – the proverbial canary in the coalmine, if you like – and that some sort of corrective action needs to be taken. Whereas in particular attention mode, your *BGIs* provide the key information needed to move a project – or your whole organisation – to the next phase of your strategy.

Either way, the maximum value from your *BGIs* comes when they're being used to serve the growth of the business. This, in turn, will only happen if the *BGI* being collected drives learning, both overall and in the context of a specific strategy.

When Do You Collect BGIs?

BGIs are ultimately only useful for the story they tell you. So we recommend that all measures are collected consistently and methodically within the *Plan-Do-Review* framework (see Chapter 13), which not only helps you to learn but also to lead. Crucially, it enables you to recognise and communicate the underlying patterns your *BGIs* create, rather than just react to the most recent output.

In short, *BGIs* relate to all aspects of *Plan-Do-Review* and not just the *Review* part. Rather, you formulate the *BGIs* in the *Plan* part, collect them in the *Do* part, and then use them to measure success (or not) and so learn from them in the *Review* part.

How Do You Maximise The Usefulness Of Your BGIs?

BGIs are meant to be useful but you can collect so many measures that they end up confusing you rather than offering clarity. So it's helpful to define, collect and analyse them within the context of specific frameworks. While by no means exhaustive, we suggest the following:

External Frameworks

- *Traditional financial accounts* – that present your financial measures of success.
- *Social Impact Report* – an annual report that focuses on the social rather than financial value you've created. For many this will be founded on your *Theory of Change* (see Appendix 1)
- *B Corp Scorecard* – a benchmarking tool of best practice for organisations looking to maximise the positive impact they have on all their stakeholders (see Appendix 1).
- *Social Enterprise Mark* - An internationally available accreditation that provides external verification that an organisation operates primarily to impact society and/or the environment positively (see Appendix 1)

Internal Frameworks

- *Overall Business Plan* – you choose the top five *BGIs* that will guide you as the leader. These will include both financial and social measures.
- *Strategy on a Page* – the key measures for every plan can be summarised within the context of the *SOAP* page.

- *The Weekly Scorecard* – a set of BGIs for your senior team that can be reviewed on a regular basis (see Chapter 15).
- *Impact Filters* – as described in the next chapter, on *Clarity of Execution*.

'Cash is the oxygen of your business so you have to watch its supply and build in the processes to make sure you are always on top of your cash situation.'

Craig Dearden Phillips, Founder, *Social Club* and *Social Minds*

How Do You Develop Your BGIs?

To start to develop your *BGIs* you have to answer the question, *What will tell us that our strategy is working?* The precise numbers then depend on what measure you decide is relevant to that particular strategy. While it sounds simple, getting to the right answer can be anything but. So, for clarity, let's for a moment go back to the beginning.

Strategy on a *Page* starts with you defining your *Purpose, Vision and Values,* and then your *Market Positioning*, all the time keeping a laser-like focus on your customer; on their problems and needs, which your enterprise has been set up to meet.

So, you have to ask yourself – in the context of the overall strategic plan – what five or six numbers will tell you that the overall strategy is working, that your organisation is fulfilling its social purpose in a sustainable way.

A good place to start is to consider measures of success for all the key stakeholders, starting with customers but including employees, investors, suppliers and the wider community you serve. Without happy customers, the money to pay your bills, employees to deliver your services, suppliers to support you and a community to serve, you'll struggle to survive, so what exactly tells you how you're doing?

Be ruthless.

You can come up with a long list of measures but, just as in flying a plane, your job is to provide direction for everyone. So you must be clear in the hierarchy of numbers you choose, both the ones that you as a leader you will use to guide the whole organisation and the areas that can be delegated to those with more specific expertise and responsibilities.

'Be Impact led - love the data as it will tell you everything,
including the things you don't want to hear,
and always give you right direction to go.'

Matt Stevenson Dodd, Founder, *Trust Impact Ltd*

Where Does Measuring Social Impact Fit In?

One of things that makes a *4th Sector* enterprise different is its commitment to social impact but this can easily get lost when considering measurement. To avoid this pitfall, you have to ensure you're clearly able to answer this basic question:

What positive change do we want to help bring about for which group of people and how and why will our intervention work?

This is often referred to as developing a *Theory of Change (TOC). (See Appendix 1.)*

Once you're clear about your *Theory of Change* you need to test it, which means you have to develop some measures that will show whether you've been successful or not. It's these measures that need to feature, front and centre, in your suite of *BGIs,* so that they're included in the day-to-day thinking of everyone in your organisation.

How Can You Support A Culture Of Measurement?

It's all very well for you to be clear about your *BGIs*, but there's a fine lie between a positive use of numbers and a damaging, target-driven culture where numbers are manipulated to keep people happy or game the system. We've all been in situations where the wrong thing is being measured and or is being used to blame and punish people for something over which they have no control.

Unsurprisingly, this creates a culture of negativity about numbers, where people run away from measurement rather than embracing it.

How can you address this? Here are four simple suggestions:

- Lead the way by being seen to use measures positively and with careful consideration. This includes investing in your own comfort with numbers by developing your knowledge and skills, not just in accounting but also in the basics of statistics.[35]
- Ensure ownership by supporting people in defining, collecting and analysing their own measures of success, within the context of the overall BGIs and their areas of responsibility.
- Openly address how measures can be misused to blame and punish rather than as a way of learning, and allow people to challenge numbers that they feel are being abused.
- Challenge people who laugh nervously and say, *I don't do numbe*rs in a tone they would never use in saying *I can't read.* In so many cases, this attitude comes from a bad past experience with maths and you need to respond to it in exactly the same positive, constructive way you would if someone said that they couldn't read.

'Don't over complicate the impact reporting. Start the work, let it teach you and things will become clearer and easier.'

Vinay Nair, Co-Founder and CEO, *Lightful*

Summary

An effective enterprise needs to measure stuff to know that it's being effective.

A key role for you as a leader is to support a culture of measurement, where clear numbers tell everyone how effectively they're doing in serving the purpose of the organisation. This starts by you deciding on a handful of measures that you can use as an instrument panel to guide you in steering your organisation towards fulfilling this purpose successfully.

We call these measures *Business Growth Indicators (BGIs),* which in simple terms, are the numbers that will tell you at a glance that your strategy is working; that you're solving the problem your customers need you to solve.

At the same time your *BGIs* also include measures of success for all the key stakeholders who form part of your social impact, including employees, investors, suppliers and the wider community.

Once you decide on your *BGIs*, all other measures – called *Key Performance Indicators (KPIs)* – can be agreed for each and every process, thus providing context for every person in any area of responsibility.

Finally to be conscious as a leader to promote numbers being used in a positive way rather than to blame or punish.

Exercise – The Hammock Test[36]

Imagine yourself sitting in a hammock on a beach. You receive a report from your office on your laptop (there's a good Wi-Fi signal!) showing the latest BGIs and the trend over the last twelve months.

What picture would that give you about the current health of your organisation? What does that say about how you're leading your company? How would it make you feel? And what two things could you do to improve things?

Chapter 13
Principle 6:
Clarity of Execution

Introduction

The aspects of clarity highlighted in our first five Principles are all essential for effectively creating a company culture that will drive growth of social impact – but they're of little use without effective execution.

This requires clear delegation of responsibilities and accountability for delivery.

Strategy on a Page (see Chapter 7) offers a framework for effective execution by making it clear and easy to delegate and communicate within the organisation.

Key to this is the process of defining the *Purpose, Vision and Values (PVV)* for the organisation. This makes it easier to map out a clear direction of travel for everyone and also helps you take the right decisions about *Talent*. Having people who understand and fit the requirements of their position, within the overall *PVV* of your enterprise, is key to them being happy to be held accountable.

Simply put, you need to build a structure where there are clear lines of accountability that state two basic points:

(i) who is responsible for the execution of each aspect of the strategy of your organisation; and

(ii) what success looks like for each of those people.

To help with this we recommend adopting three connected tools:

1. The Impact Filter
2. The Plan-Do-Review Cycle
3. Flowcharting

Exercise

Think of an element of your strategy for your enterprise that you have delegated to a senior person in your team that didn't work out successfully.

Give yourself a score out of 10 for how well you feel you executed the delegation?

As the delegator what could you have done to improve this score by 2?

How does that make you feel?

The Impact Filter

We learned about the *Impact Filter (See Fig 13.1)* from its inventor, Dan Sullivan of *Strategic Coach*, who developed it to provide an effective bridge between the deeper thinking that goes into working on the business and the detailed execution demanded by working in the business on a specific project.

Why Is An Impact Filter So Helpful In Driving Accountability And Execution?

An *Impact Filter* helps its user (often you but also other people) gain clarity on why a specific project or even a completely new idea is worth committing to and then communicating this clarity to everyone who's relevant to the project's delivery or the idea's development. It offers a simple checklist that helps to road test and mould what might be a vague concept into something with a clearly defined direction of travel and clear criteria for success. It also summarises everything in a way that makes it easy to sell to anyone else who might be needed to achieve success.

What Exactly Is An Impact Filter?

An *Impact Filte*r is both a tool and a thinking process. The format contains the following key elements, which also dovetail with *Strategy on a Page:*

- *Heading* - The name of the project; the owner of the *Impact Filter* (the person who is leading the project or who has the idea) and the date it was created
- *Foundations questions* – the project's *Purpose,* its *Importance* and its *Ideal Outcome*
- *Best and Worst Results* – what you foresee if you do or don't take action
- *Success Criteria* – the things (specially the numbers) that will tell you that the project has been a success

The Impact Filter

Project: ______ Owner: ______ Date: ______

		Success Criteria (What has to be true when this project is finished?)
Purpose (What do you want to achieve?)		
Importance (What's the biggest difference this will make?)		
Ideal Outcome (What does the completed project look like?)		

Best Result (If you do take action)	
Worst Result (If you don't take action)	

Figure 13.1: The Impact Filter

Who Uses The Impact Filter?

It starts with you but is easy for anyone to use. So, once you're confident and can clearly model its use, it's a very practical delegation tool to empower your team to think through and communicate their own ideas and projects.

When Is It Used?

An *Impact Filter* can be used when initially considering and developing any idea or project and then again when reviewing it. But as Dan Sullivan emphasises, you only share your *Impact Filter* once you've really gone through it thoroughly and are fully committed to the idea. 'If you're not sold,' he says, 'don't try and sell it.' When you are, though, you'll be ready to communicate the *Impact Filter* to the people who you need to get the job done, to empower them to support you.

Where Is It Used?

An Impact Filter can be used wherever there is something that can be defined as a project. This could range from a simple meeting to a major organisation-wide initiative.

How Is It Used?

An *Impact Filter* is generally developed and used in a series of steps:

- *Step 1* – Spend no more that half an hour to complete the filter. The intention is to develop it to the point where you're clear and confident about using it to communicate the idea to whoever else needs to be involved in putting it into action.
- *Step 2* - Consider their input and adjust the filter accordingly.
- *Step 3* – Once everyone is agreed, you use the amended *Impact Filter* to develop a more detailed plan or to delegate this process to someone else.
- *Step 4* – Use it as a point of reference during the review process once the project is completed.

What Are The Key Elements Of The Impact Filter?

The *Impact Filter* asks five key questions that help communicate why a project is worth doing.

1. *What's the Purpose?* Why are you doing it? What do you want to achieve specifically? How does this relate to the purpose of one of your *SOAP* pages and in turn to the overall organisational *Purpose?*

2. *Why is it so important?* What is the biggest difference achieving this purpose will make to your enterprise's overall *Purpose?* Why will things be better as a result of doing this and why will everyone involved be better off as a result of participating in it? Consider where you are right now and then where things will be when the project is finished. What is the measurable difference between these two points? How important/valuable is this difference?

3. *What's the Ideal Outcome?* Here you state your vision of the project's best possible outcome. What does it look like? How vivid and inspiring is it?

4. *Best and Worst Results?* What's the best result if you do take action on the idea and the worst result if you don't. Defining these creates a picture of two extreme outcomes. By writing down how you'll feel if you achieve your vision of the project's success – or if you fail to – you're able to rehearse both outcomes and build your determination to succeed; to believe that there is no alternative but to go ahead. In other words, for a project to work it needs to make sense not just to your brain but to your heart and your instincts. Once you've completed a picture of two completely different potential outcomes you should be fully invested in following through on the idea. If you're not, you really have to ask yourself whether it's worthwhile.

5. *Success Criteria?* As Dan Sullivan says, 'The simplest and most efficient way to ensure you get the results you want is to create a list of success criteria for your project.' These outline what the project looks like when it's done and done well. They also act as a checklist for everyone involved, to make sure they're on the right track towards achieving the outcome you're looking for.

It's helpful to visualise your project when it's 100% completed and write down a list of all the things you want to be true about it on that day. And remember that vagueness generates vagueness, so make sure that you write down specific numbers or specific events – things that when your project is completed will be clearly true or not true, rather than something imprecise and ambiguous.

The Plan-Do-Review Cycle

'Don't wait for perfection - do it, reflect and refine - learn by doing rather than waiting around for everything to be perfect.'

Celia Hodson, Founder, *Hey Girls*

Why Is The Plan-Do-Review Cycle A Core Accountability Tool?

As a leader you need to drive action and keep things moving, but in the quest to get things done it's often tempting to rush planning, devote every ounce of energy to the doing and regard reviewing what has happened as a luxury you never quite get round to because there's just too much to do. This can often prove to be a false economy, as a lot of effort can be expended with little productive output – apart from frustration.

That's why we place so much emphasis on the *Plan-Do-Review (PDR) Cycle*, a simple but highly effective tool that gives equal weight to all three stages.

Proper planning means that the time spent doing is well-spent, while reviewing checks the plan against the outcome and feeds that learning back into future planning and action.

Additionally, making *PDR* a habit ensures clarity in how projects are put into action, who takes responsibility for what and, crucially, how learning takes place.

Exercise

There's a famous military adage – *No plan survives first contact with the enemy.*[37] In other words, there's always something to be learnt from the execution of every plan, and how wasteful it would be not to capture that learning and put it to good use in the future. The energy and enthusiasm that's generated when people are learning and improving can so easily evaporate when you're going around the same old stuff every day.

So, before we look at PDR in detail, take a moment to write down something that you've learnt recently as part of a work project you were responsible for. How did you manage this responsibility and reflect on the process that delivered the learning?

Then think back to the original plan and write down two things you'd change in the light of that learning.

What Is Plan-Do-Review (PDR)?

Well, the clue is in the name. *Plan-Do-Review* are the key steps that have to happen, in that order, for an activity not just to be completed successfully but also to be improved. In simple terms, *PDR* is a doing-and-learning process.

To break it down – based on your initial understanding of any activity or challenge – first you plan what you want to do, then you do it, and then you monitor and review the result of doing it. This new understanding – or learning – is then fed into an updated plan as the cycle starts over again. That is, *Plan-Do-Review* isn't a one-off process. It's regular and repeated and can be applied to any activity. So, it can quickly become a powerful feature of your organisational culture.

When Is Plan-Do-Review Used?

PDR can be used all the time. Its simplicity allows it to be applied to any task, from the smallest plan to the biggest, and by one person or two, or a whole team of people. The scale and complexity will change with the size of the task but the *Plan-Do-Review* steps are always the same. And it drives execution by holding the owner of the plan accountable not just for success but also for the delivery of learning towards a desired outcome.

Who Is Involved In Plan-Do-Review?

Everyone is involved in *PDR*. Too often people think that planning is only for managers but the key to effective execution – i.e. the doing of *PDR* – is that everyone in the organisation is using *PDR* at any level, for any task, at any scale. By weaving it into the daily fabric of your enterprise in this way, your learning, innovation and effectiveness as an organisation can only improve.

Exercise

Think of a recent work project.

How might it have been improved if certain key people who weren't involved had been included in the planning, doing or reviewing?

Try to identify at least one improvement for each of the three stages.

How Do You Make A Plan?

It sounds like a simple question but it's not as obvious as it seems – because the real question is *How do you make a good plan?* Or tougher still, *How do you make the right plan, the one that's going to ensure you get the best possible result?* Surprisingly, the answer is given in this famous poem by Rudyard Kipling.

I keep six honest serving-men
(They taught me all I knew);
Their names are What and Why and When
And How and Where and Who.

What, Why, When, How, Where and *Who* – believe it or not, you can create any plan by answering those questions. In most cases you can even create it on a single page; but if that's not possible – because the task is too complex, say – the *Six Honest Serving-Men* stay the same and the answers simply require more detail.

Step 1 Why

Always start with *Why* – the basic purpose of the task; then ask the *What, Who, When* and *Where* in that order; and only at the end do you dive into the detailed *How?*. But also ask *Why?* at the end of each question to double check that everything relates to the original purpose – *What-Why, Who-Why,* and so on.

As we've seen in the discussion on *Purpose, Vision and Values,* Why is the question that goes to the heart of everything your organisation does. It's the question that ensures that every plan, no matter how small, will be grounded in your original purpose as a enterprise. After all, if isn't tied to that original purpose, isn't serving it in some way, then what is the point of expending time and energy to do it?

A word of warning, though. If your answer to *Why?* is a long description that sets out more than one purpose, you probably need to simplify things till you've got real clarity. Maybe your task is too complicated or is trying to hit too many goals, or needs to be broken down into distinct stages. A single sentence of ten words or less is ideal as it pushes you to be disciplined and grounded in your thinking and planning; to define, refine, then redefine the purpose – until you've got it right.

Exercise

Consider a recent project that didn't work and give it a mark out of 10 for how clear you think its agreed purpose was to everyone involved.

Then consider how that could be improved by 2 points.

Now use that to articulate the purpose of your current project in a sentence of ten words or less.

What Are The Next Steps And In What Order?

Step 2 What?

Once you're clear on why you're undertaking this task and how it relates to the core purpose of your enterprise, you need to answer the *What?* question. Or rather questions, plural, because one *What?* tends to lead to another – and eventually to lots of *What's?* So it can be really helpful to organise all these under three basic questions.

- *'What is the goal of this task?'* Be precise about what you intend to achieve and keep this clearly in view at all times.
- *'What non-physical resources do you need to achieve it?'* This means things like knowledge, understanding, relationships – things you can't physically touch but which are crucial to you reaching the goal. This prompts two related questions – what non-physical resources do you already have and so what are the gaps?
- *'What physical resources do you need to achieve the goal?'* Everything from paperclips to people to industrial plant. Again, you also need to ask what physical resources you already have and what the gaps are.

Don't forget, too, that relating the *Whats?* back to the *Why?* is also essential to this repeated process of achieving clarity.

Step 3 Who?

It's sometimes said about films and plays that casting is all. Cast the right actors and your problems are solved. Obviously, it's more complicated than that but there's still a lot of truth in the principle that getting the right people involved in your task, in the right roles, is a key element in achieving your goals. That means the right people internally and, as far as you can manage it, externally. So, the *Who?* question can be broken down into those two categories.

- First, who internally – inside your enterprise – should be involved in the planning? Who is in charge overall? Who should be kept informed, who should be consulted, who should do what?
- Second, externally, who else needs to be involved? Who needs to know about the plan, who should be consulted, asked to advise, invited to give feedback, even invited to join the team? And crucially, of course, who is the customer? Or more precisely, who's paying for this and – if they're different – who is the actual end-user?

Again, don't forget to add the *Why?* question. Why are you involving these people, internally and externally? This relates back to the purpose of this task and, ultimately, back to the core purpose of your enterprise.

Step 4 When?

The *When?* question is all about schedules, timelines and timings. It's about asking when things need to be done, in what order and by when. And again, it's about asking why – why this order of events, this schedule and these dates?

The *When?* question can actually be quite brutal – in a good way – because it injects the discipline of deadlines into your task planning and execution.

The simplest way to go about answering *When?* is to set provisional start and end dates – which might be very precise or very approximate, depending on the task. Then put in sequence every separate mini-task that has to happen between them, paying close attention to whatever needs to happen for – or before – something else can then happen.

This is important because it lets you spot potential bottlenecks that could slow down or even derail the whole task. Everything might hinge on a person or a package or a piece of information arriving at a precise time, for example, and if it doesn't ...

So, when you have the sequence laid out you can estimate how much time each of those mini-tasks is going to need, and which of them can be tackled in parallel. Then – and only then – do you start to put actual dates to everything. At this point you can see if your task is going to be possible between your start and end dates, and where adjustments might have to be made – moving certain dates, say, or bringing in more people to get the job done on time, or maybe even rethinking the whole plan.

Step 5 Where?

When you're planning *Where?* is a question that can sound simple, straightforward – innocent even. Don't be deceived. *Where?* is the question that often forces your lovely, intricate plan to confront the cold, hard facts of physical reality.

Where is our key supplier located? A thousand miles away. Oh. And the implications of that are...?

Where are we actually going to set up shop? All the options are beyond our budget, so...?

Even *Where are we going to put everyone?* We haven't got a room big enough...

In other words, nice plan meets physical reality. So, the *Why?* of *Where?* is that it's a great reality-check question – as in *OK, lovely idea. But where are we going to find the 350 customers we need each week to make us viable...?*

So how can you make sure that you don't miss any of these vital *Where?* questions in your planning?

One way is to use the timeline you created in answering the When? question. A key feature of that process is putting in sequence every separate mini-task that has to happen for the main task to be fulfilled. So, using that sequence, you can simply ask where each of these mini-tasks is going to take place, which can reveal all sorts of useful information.

Step 6 How?

For your planning process you start with a $64,000 question – *Why?* Why are you doing any of this? And you end with another one – *How?* How do you actually tackle, solve, address all of the challenges that – thanks to the five other *Honest Serving-Men* – you've identified as relevant to completing your current project?

This is when the team you've assembled in answering the *Who?* question has to come into its own. Together, you have to draw on your collective experience and creativity to overcome all the problems and difficulties that stand between you and success. And if your team can't do this, you have to cast your net wider to find the people who can.

This means that the *How?* question must include planning how and what you're going to measure to judge your progress, honestly and accurately. These markers can be collected regularly during the doing stage and used in the review stages of the *PDR* process to give the basis for ongoing learning.

How Do You Measure Progress?

To measure your progress, it helps to break things down into three categories – *quantity, quality* and *time.*

Quantity measures are anything that you can count or put a number to – customers served, widgets made, units sold, that sort of thing.

Quality measures are basically subjective. They're mostly about opinions, judgments, preferences – what you might get from a customer survey, for example. Though also note that some measures of quality are actually judged by quantity, something that can be counted; for instance, 24 carat (or pure gold) is of a higher quality than 9 carat gold, which is less than 50% pure.

Time measures relate to progress against the timeline, to show whether or not you've hit certain markers in the schedule, to the required standard and by the set date.

These measures work separately and in combination.

So, for example, a customer survey could measure how many people (quantity) judge your product or service as good, bad or indifferent (quality) at regular periods during its development (time). Are you winning more people over – or maybe losing them?

The *measurement and evaluation (M&E)* of your progress in any task, and of the ultimate impact you're having in fulfilling your social Purpose, can be straightforward – or anything but.

So, designing the right *M&E* framework could be something you can do yourself or it might be something for which you need external input.

The Key Tip For Doing

We focus a lot in the *PDR* process on the *Plan* phase and the *Review* phase, so that the *Do* phase is as simple as it can be. When you've put in the time and effort to produce a really well thought-through plan, it will lay out for you everything that needs to be done, by whom, in what order and to what timeline. And – crucially – it'll include how to monitor, measure and review the task so that adjustments can be made as necessary and everything's kept moving towards completion.

In short, *The Plan* is king.

So, the key tip for the *Do* part is obvious – *stick to the plan!*

Are All Reviews The Same?

The simple answer is no, all reviews are not the same. They differ according to when they're carried out and how wide-ranging or specific they are.

For example, periodic and concurrent reviews are the regular and ad hoc reviews that you conduct during the task. These tend to focus on certain key numbers and/or key aspects to ensure that everything is on track and prompt whatever changes might be needed.

By contrast, post-reviews are conducted after the task's been completed and you want to reflect on how everyone has done. If you've already built short, sharp and regular task reviews into your working routine – so that they become a habit, almost like a coffee break - a post-review doesn't have to be the all-singing, all-dancing comprehensive assessment that many people dread for a lot of tasks. Thankfully, the periodic and concurrent reviews you've built into your timeline will ensure that a post-review can be carried out with a lot less stress and angst.

In fact, it can even be useful to have a structured pre-review at the very beginning of your planning process, where you're able to gather together previous learnings and apply them to the planning phase itself. This enables the objectives, focus and strategy to be questioned.

When Do You Review?

While all reviews are not the same you do need to review frequently. Our experience suggests that the usual balance tends to be 80% doing, 10% planning and 10% reviewing, with the reviewing often being done only when things go badly wrong.

Ideally, though, the split should be about even. Short, sharp review meetings should be held on a regular (periodic) basis, with ad hoc (concurrent) reviews conducted as needed to look at specific issues; and the post-review organised to reflect on everything at the end of the task.

Who Should Be Involved In The Review?

The people who should be involved in the review basically depends on the type of review.

For a pre-review you might involve just your initial core team, which could then grow as a direct result of that review – a lesson learned from a previous project might be that you need a greater range of planning input. For a regular, weekly half-hour *Progress, Issues and Next Steps* review (see *How to review* below) it might be enough to involve just the key people who are managing the doing of the task. And for a full-on, let's-put-it-all-out there, post-task review you might want to include anyone – everyone – who's had any input to the project at any point.

As a rule of thumb, though, everyone involved in the planning process should be involved in the review process.

That means both everyone internal to your enterprise and everyone external to it, too – so customers, suppliers, consultants, the person in the legal department at the local council; basically, whoever had some degree of involvement. The thinking is that if they added value at the planning stage, their reflections could add something to the review process, too.

And don't forget the doers. Often, they can offer the most crucial insights of all because they're the ones who've actually had to put your plans into action – and have maybe encountered issues you and your planning team had never imagined.

Involving as many people as possible in the post-review process doesn't mean trying to jam them all into a meeting-room at the same time and asking them what they think. There are lots of different ways that you can get feedback – one-to-one, in smaller meetings, online, in surveys; where there's a will there's a way. And, of course, you don't have to do it all in one go – there should be a clearly defined review period, the more structured the better, as we explore next.

How To Review – 3 + 3 = Review

To get the maximum value from your review process you need to do it thoroughly and consistently, and the best way to do that is to stick to a simple but rigorous template. We suggest *3+3 = Review.*

The first 3 refers to the three essential questions you need to ask as summarised by the acronym *PIN – Progress-Issues-Next* (steps):

- What *Progress* have we made? And what measures are we using to tell us that?
- What *Issues* have come up? Meaning what obstacles, challenges, problems and so on, especially ones that we didn't anticipate.
- And what are the *Next* steps we should take?

The next three refer to what you need to ask those three questions about, namely:

- The *Task* itself – that is, what you're trying to achieve and have achieved; in other words, what you're actually doing.
- The *Process* - how you work together, your structure, relationships, decision-making, communication and so on.
- And the *Learning* – the knowledge and experience you've gained, individually and as a team, from doing this task i.e. any new ideas, understandings, opportunities, people; things like that.

When you review, you can apply *PIN* specifically to *Task, Process or Learning*, one at a time, or review them all together. It's up to you and the demands of your plan. Wherever possible, though, it's best to use a clear measure of success identified in the planning phase rather than just guesswork to mark your progress, identify issues and set targets for your next steps.

Flowcharting

Why Is Flowcharting Useful?

While *SOAP* is helpful for allocating areas of responsibility, there are times when you might be unclear about how to go about doing things in the most effective way; for example, there can be confusion about who should do what and when in delivering the service to its final customer. The result is inefficiency and sometimes complete failure in fulfilling your enterprise's overall *Purpose.*

Flowcharting is a great way to clarify the design of the most effective way to deliver your product or service. It's a process that lays out each step – from a customer's point of view – in order to maximise your resources of time, energy and money and deliver in a manner that doesn't just delight the customer but all of the other stakeholders, too.

Flowcharting with the people involved in delivery, from beginning to end, is the most constructive way to proceed. It'll help you clarify any confusion, diagnose what factors influence performance, expose areas of complexity, misunderstanding and inconsistency and delegate responsibilities for solutions.

From a leadership point of view, flowcharting is particularly useful in helping you understand problems and challenges that may be remote from your day-to day-work, so that you and the people directly involved can explore potential solutions together.

What Is Flowcharting?

As its name suggests, a flowchart is a visual representation of the flow of an activity – from start to finish – using a combination of words and symbols. Put simply, a flowchart shows what happens as a result of something else happening.

For example here is a flowchart of a leader going through the *Bubble Chamber* 13 week clarity programme.

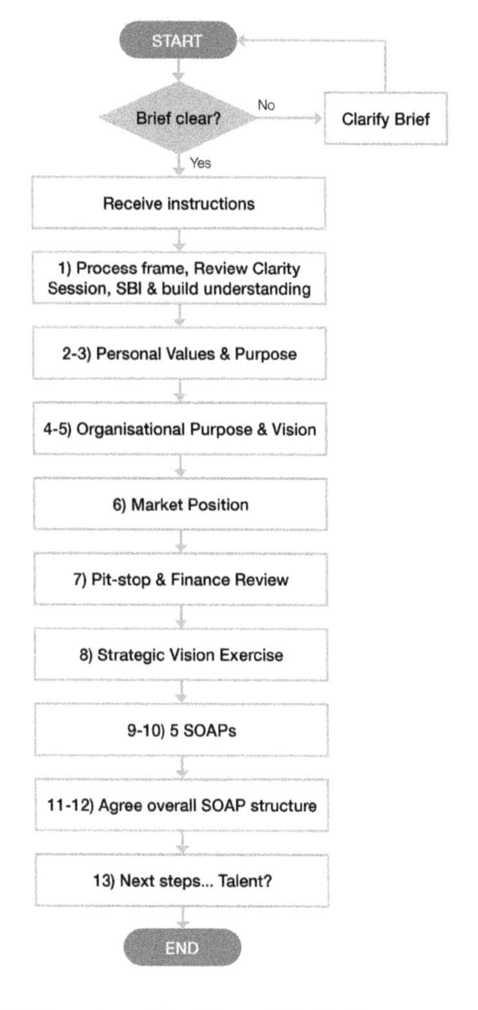

Figure 13.2 Mars view of the 13-week Clarity Programme from a leaders point of view

When Are Flowcharts Useful?

Flowcharts can be used in a wide range of settings. While they're commonly used in manufacturing industries, they're equally useful in designing process within service industries. They offer an ideal means to explain a new idea, product or way of doing things and to understand what is going on, clarify thoughts and understand how to improve any existing process at work or at home. And key to the effective use of flowcharting is to keep the point of view of the customer/end-user front and centre at all times.

Who Should Be Involved In Flowcharting?

Flowcharting is most definitely best done by a group of people directly involved in delivering the process being flow-charted. A common error is for a single person, distanced from the end result, to draw up a flowchart based on an assumption of reality which has little, or even no resemblance to what is actually taking place on the ground.

Five Top Tips For Effective Flowcharting Illustrated By Our Example

It is easy to end up getting bogged down in too much detail when drawing a flowcharting and as with all tools, it can take a bit of practice but you will ensure you make a positive start if you begin by following these five tips:

1. Every flowchart needs to have a title explaining the purpose of what is being charted. In the case of our example its purpose is *To flowchart the 13 week leader programme...*

2. Every flowchart should state the level on which it's being viewed and from whose point of view. Our example explains it is at *....the Mars (or highest) view..... and from the leaders point of view*

3. Be clear with every flowchart where it starts and where it ends. As a rule-of-thumb, no flowchart should have more than ten actions/symbols.

4. If you find that you have more than ten you need to collate a series of actions into a shadow box that indicates another level of detail, which will need to be flowcharted on another chart. It's useful when drawing each different level of detail to give them clear labels in the title of the flowchart to indicate where they fit into the bigger picture.

5. If the chart involves more than a single person or team, it's useful to lay it out in columns where each column is headed by the name of the person responsible for the actions it contains. That way responsibilities can be clearly seen and allocated.

Summary

In this chapter we've focused on how you can lay the foundations for a clear culture of accountability for execution.

We've introduced three tools – *The Impact Filter,* the *Plan-Do-Review Cycle* and *Flowcharting* – to help everyone, from you as leader right down to your frontline staff, develop a common language and way of working to support this process.

Exercise

Revisit the project that you visualised at the beginning of this chapter and consider which of the three tools we've covered in this chapter might increase the score you originally gave for its execution by two.

However good they are, though, tools don't work by themselves. Integral to the successful application of each tool are our last two Principles – *Measurement and Communication.*

Chapter 14
Principle 7: Clarity of Communication

'We've got a big problem, we human beings. Bigger than plastic in the oceans and toxins in the air, bigger even than climate change. It's how we talk and listen to each other.'

Peter Osborn and Eddy Canfor-Dumas, *The Talking Revolution*[38]

Introduction

Conflict.

Hands up anyone who likes it.

In truth, not many of us – and most people say they avoid it like the plague.

On the other hand, think about a conflict, perhaps with your Board or a member of your Senior Leadership Team, that you now regret you avoided. What was the effect on you on others and on the conflict itself?

Did the conflict and the emotions you felt about turn inwards and come out again in some other way? Losing a client or contract, for example, or not sleeping or even quitting a job you love perhaps?

How much did this cost you in terms of energy, pain – and simply hard cash? Alongside the many hidden costs of poor communication and misunderstanding, lots of research[39] shows the other side of the coin – that good relationships, based on good communication, make us happier and more productive.

So this chapter presents our seventh and final Principle, the one that arguably holds the other six together and failing to master will mean that any leader is destined to suffer endless frustration. It focuses on how you can help yourself and your organisation by developing clear and effective habits of communication to turn the conflicts we run from into opportunities for creativity and positive change.

It's perhaps the best ROI you will ever achieve.

What Is A Creative Conversation?

The Talking Revolution describes *creative conversation* as an approach that *'actively seeks to create something of value in every conversation ... the type of verbal exchange that enriches and energises us, that clears our minds and even uplifts us... [It] can range from a simple chat to a life-changing dialogue - it's the quality that counts.'*

In this section we will introduce the seven key elements of creative conversation as defined in *The Talking Revolution:*

- The Three Attitudes of Personal Responsibility, Openness and Creativity
- The Three Practices of Understanding, Challenging and Being Understood
- The art of Conversation Management that integrates the other six

Mastering any one of these will have a significant impact on the effectiveness of your communication. Mastering all seven will be transformative.

But why these? Well, together they form the nuts and bolts of normal, everyday interaction at work. They permeate the whole business and, as leaders, our own individual approach to these things – with colleagues, customers, suppliers and the wider world – significantly impacts the culture of the enterprise. It's crucial to get this right, as it's sadly common for low level conflict just to be accepted as a fact of working life. This can be hugely expensive in terms of productivity, job satisfaction and ultimately whether or not you achieve your purpose as an enterprise. But it doesn't have to be that way.

What Is Conflict And Why Should We Care?

Conflict, large and small, occurs all the time – inside organisations, and externally with suppliers, customers, funders and neighbours.

But what's at the heart of it? The answer, surprisingly, is that conflict arises from caring. Here's a definition we use.

Conflict occurs when people perceive, correctly or not, that something they care about is being threatened or denied.

The something that people care about can be very concrete or much more subtle – like people needing respect or consideration. It signals that you have to pay attention to something the other person cares about, because a threat to or denial of that 'something' is the spark to a process that can easily grow ...

The good news is that we're all able to do something about such situations because the way we communicate and address conflict is just a set of habits we've established over time and which we can therefore change. It takes commitment and courage and an investment of time and energy, but once you commit to this change, the results come quickly – and increase the more you practise.

Exercise

Here are four questions for you to consider:

- How well do I listen to – and ensure that I've understood – others?
- How well do I express myself - and ensure that I've been understood?
- How well do I challenge people but still leave them feeling positive/invigorated?
- How well do I handle conflict or do I tend to avoid it? Or even inadvertently make it worse?

Give yourself a mark out of 10 in response to these four questions. Then, if you dare, ask a trusted friend or colleague to mark you against the same points – and compare the results…

'We need to think about conflict as an energy, as a force rather than as something to be scared of and something that can actually be the source of huge creativity and change and a positive force for good.'

Jo Broadwood, CEO *Cohesion & Integration Network*

The Three Attitudes Of Personal Responsibility, Openness And Creativity

This section covers three basic attitudes that work together to guide your communication approach. Using them to become conscious of how you behave gives you a compass for achieving the best possible result for any communication. So what do they involve?

1. Personal Responsibility

Taking personal responsibility means to understand that you are at the centre of your own unique communication network and that any changes you make in your communication behaviour – in your thoughts, feelings, words, tone and actions – will inevitably affect to some degree the other people in that network. This includes taking full responsibility for your reactions to other people.

For example, it's very common to point the finger and say *He makes me so angry!* when he is simply behaving in a way that you don't like. Personal responsibility means saying, *When he does that I get so angry!* It's a small but significant difference that actually empowers you. By taking responsibility for how you feel, this becomes something that you can control, manage and then use to guide the conversation in a productive direction.

2. Openness

Openness relates to your attitude to others and what they care about. It calls for you to suspend your judgemental reflex and replace it with a habit to understand first, even if you don't agree with what you're hearing. Any challenge you want to make can come later, based on that understanding.

Openness is a highly pragmatic attitude because people respond best when they feel heard and understood, not just about specific facts but particularly about their core values, what they feel is really important to them. If these values aren't acknowledged they tend to close down or even become hostile. Being open means you take responsibility to do this initial understanding, regardless of your own views.

The rewards are significant.

3. Creativity

Creativity is the attitude that describes how you approach the inevitable twists and turns of the conversation that are created when you take personal responsibility for it and remain open. It's the attitude that's always looking for the possibility to create something of value, to fashion something new and unique that arises from the safe space where emotions can be expressed, ideas explored, options examined and solutions co-created without the fear of dismissive judgement.

The table below, taken from *The Talking Revolution,* splits some common behaviours into those that are creative and those that are non-creative or, worse, destructive. See which ones you can spot yourself other people doing.

Creativity	Non-Creativity
Empathises	Distances, judges, condemns
Clarifies	Confuses, obscures, misrepresents
Explores	Lacks curiosity, ignores, withdraws
Opens up	Closes down, defends, denies
Conveys respect	Belittles, insults, mocks

Figure 14.1: Creative and Non-Creative Attitudes

Of course, living these attitudes can be testing, especially when something we care about and in which we're emotionally invested is challenged in some way. This is why it's so important that the Three Attitudes are supported by and expressed through the Three Practices.

The Three Practices Of Understanding, Challenging And Being Understood

While the *Three Attitudes* express the basic spirit with which to approach creative conversation, the *Three Practices* are the basic actions through which you can apply this spirit in your everyday interactions with other people. Let's look at them each in turn.

1. Understanding

Understanding is about developing the discipline in any conversation of focusing on, and achieving clarity about what the other person is saying. As Steven Covey says in his book, *The 7 Habits of Highly Effective People*, 'Seek first to understand before seeking to be understood.'

It's generally thought that good communication depends on the skills of the person who's telling others what they think – the *transmitter.* The reality is the complete opposite. The most powerful person in any conversation is actually the *listener* – the *receiver.*

If you find this hard to believe, try a little experiment. In your next conversation, start by showing real interest in the other person as they speak but become more and more distracted, until you're showing no interest at all. Unless the speaker is completely self-absorbed, they'll find it increasingly difficult to keep talking and might even get quite offended. One way or another, we feel demotivated if we think the person we're talking to isn't listening, especially if what we're trying to say is important to us.

This means that in any conversation it's in the listener's hands to empower or disempower the speaker – in a creative conversation it's the former we're aiming for, of course – and this is done by focusing explicitly on striving to understand what's being transmitted.

What Makes A Good Understander?

A good understander is certainly a good listener but goes further. They pay attention, listen with an open mind, clarify what they're hearing and then summarise it to ensure that what's now in their head is an accurate reflection of what's in the other person's. Whether they agree or not is another story, but they've consciously put their own opinion on hold while they've devoted their efforts to understanding the other person – and clearly showing that they have.

How To Understand?

We suggest that *Understanding* can be developed in three very practical stages.

Stage 1 Focus. Tune in to the other person and give them your complete attention until you've understood. Always remember that one of the things we human beings are very good at it is not saying what we mean. Disguising it. Hiding it – even from ourselves. So – often – the real issue isn't on the surface. It's underneath, in the subtext of what people are saying. In fact, often it's so deep in that subtext that even the people involved find it hard to explain exactly what's driving the conflict between them.

This is where the *PIN* iceberg can help you get to the root of what's really going on.

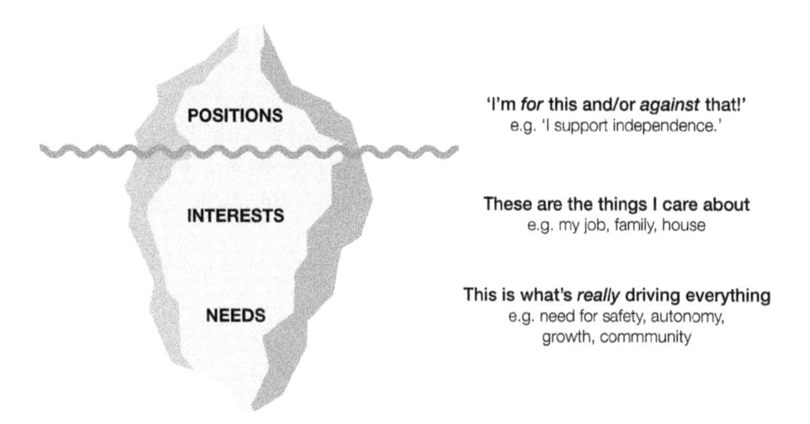

Figure 14.1: PIN Iceberg

A *Position* is like the iceberg that's visible above the water. It's the stated attitude. But underneath it are *Interests* – the specific things a person cares about that they can think are being threatened or denied. And they care about these things because, at an even deeper level, they meet some of their basic human *Needs,* as described by Tony Robbins (See p85). By identifying and understanding the interests and needs present you can explore the idea that they might be met in different ways.

Stage 2 Clarify. Clarify what you're hearing by feeding back little nuggets of understanding along the way. Be an active understander. A handy way of doing this is to use the acronym *TED – Tell, Explain, Describe.*

- Tell me about that.
- Could you explain a bit more?
- Could you describe what you saw... or felt or heard?

Stage 3 Summarise. When you think you've got the whole thing, *Summarise* it. Pull together what you've heard – not your view or your advice – just your summation of what you think the other person's saying. A useful starting point could be to use phrases like *So, what you're saying is ...* or *Let me see if I've got this right ...* . And the great thing about this is you always win.

If your summary is accurate it confirms you've understood and also provides a marker for the conversation to move on that avoids those frustrating loops of repetition. And if it's not accurate you give the other person the chance to correct you. You can't lose.

2. Challenging

Challenging is about testing what's being said in a way that opens things up and leads to greater clarity and connection, rather than shutting things down or causing an argument. But challenging what other people are saying – and being challenged by them – can make us feel uncomfortable and so it's something we often try to avoid, consciously or unconsciously. This is a problem in any enterprise, though, as an organisational culture that discourages challenge presents a significant obstacle to initiative and growth.

Of course, if handled clumsily a challenge can easily lead to conflict and ill-feeling. But done skilfully – and it's a skill anyone can learn – challenging is invaluable. It can clarify and test ideas, explore and expand possibilities, guard against assumptions and *groupthink* – and find clarity in the midst of confusion.

Exercise

Think of a time when you didn't challenge something and then regretted it.

Why didn't you challenge?

Note down what happened and why. Then write three positive things that you think might have happened if you had challenged.

What Can Be Challenged?

The *BBC* journalist John Simpson famously said of Nelson Mandela, 'He always spoke to the great person he knew you could be', which is also key to challenging in a creative conversation. The ability to challenge well, and be challenged, is essential for clarity in your organisation. But does that mean you can challenge anything? That nothing's off-limits?

Well, the rule of thumb is that it's OK to challenge the content of what someone says – the facts they present or how they interpret them, for example – but the more personal things are, the more care is needed.

So, attitudes, facts (especially how they're being interpreted), assumptions, behaviour, emotional expression and even beliefs, are completely legitimate areas for challenge. But what's a real no-no is a challenge that's simply a form of (perhaps disguised) personal criticism.

When Should You Challenge?

The short answer is, challenge when your understanding is complete and not before. We must all have been challenged at some point by someone who hasn't really understood the situation or what we're saying. Frustrating, isn't it? And all it does is add personal irritation to the stack of whatever it is that needs sorting out.

Understanding first lays the foundation for calm, two-way conversation, in which respectful challenges are easier to say and far more likely to be heard and acted upon.

How Do You Challenge?

It's been said that challenge without empathy is caustic - but empathy without challenge is anaemic and there are plenty of all-too-familiar ways to challenge poorly. Here are a few examples of *what not to do*. If you want to have some fun try out our bingo challenge game in *Appendix 2*.

- *Rejection:* 'You're just wrong.'
- *Devaluing the message:* 'That's completely irrelevant/ridiculous.'
- *Attacking the messenger:* 'You're just too sensitive/unfeeling/ dumb.'
- *Appealing to the crowd:* 'Well, you're in a minority of one if you think that!

So how can you find that sweet spot where you don't just roll over in a conversation but equally your challenge isn't so harsh that you destroy the possibility of a positive outcome? In short, how do you find the *Goldilocks Zone* where you get it just right?

Well, here are four *TIPS* for effective challenging. Try being *Tentative, Invitational, Positive* and *Specific.*

- *Tentative* challenges use *soft* phrases like *It seems to me...* and *I'm wondering whether...* and avoid aggressive or dogmatic language. In this way, they create space for the other person to retreat into, if necessary, without losing face.
- *Invitational* challenges offer suggestions to see something differently, which gives the other person the choice of accepting or declining the invitation. And it's very hard to be offended by an invitation.
- *Positive* challenges make it clear that you're working towards a mutually beneficial outcome of some kind and seek to acknowledge the positive intentions of the other person, even if they're not immediately obvious.

- *Specific* challenges avoid sweeping generalisations – *All men are…*, *No woman ever…* – and blanket accusations like *You never do such-and-such* or *You always do such-and-such.* Instead, they focus on precise details that you and the other person can examine together.

3. Being Understood

Whenever we talk to other people we tend to assume that what we say goes in a smooth, uninterrupted flow. But what is this based on? After all, we know that when it's the other way around, understanding others is not so simple – and if we're often pretty poor understanders, chances are that other people aren't so great either. Even if the person we're talking to says they've understood, how do we know that what they've taken in is actually what we intended?

Being *Understood* is about focusing on the needs of the listener to ensure that what we ourselves *transmit* is received with clarity and understanding by them. It's about consciously taking responsibility (a) to make it as easy as possible for the listener to understand you; and (b) to check – as far as you can – that they have actually understood.

Who Is Responsible For Being Understood?

When you switch from understanding someone else to being understood by them, the responsibility for clarity moves with you. In other words, you consciously take responsibility for being understood.

What this means practically is that you need to adopt different approaches according to circumstances and here is a checklist of things to consider to help you succeed.

- *Be aware* of the person you're talking to. For example:
  - What do they know already?
  - Why should they be interested in what you're about to say?
  - Is this a good/convenient time for them to have this conversation?
- *Physical setting* can play a big part in how others listen to you and can affect the degree to which you're understood.
  - Is the setting comfortable and private, for example, or noisy and full of people?
  - Is the conversation happening on their ground or yours?
  - Is it formal or informal?
  - And will they – or you – feel relaxed or tense, or maybe even a bit intimidated by the surroundings?
- *Purpose* means to make clear to the other person – ideally at its start – why you're having this conversation in the first place.
- The *Headline* puts the main thing you want to be understood in a single, short, clear sentence, as with a newspaper headline.
- *Painting the Picture* fills in the detail by giving a clear frame and enough background and foreground for the listener to make sense of what they're hearing.
- *Checking* that you've been understood prompts the other person to say something that confirms they've 'received' the key elements of what you've 'transmitted'. And it might be important to check as you go, especially if what you're saying is lengthy and/or complicated and/or important.
  - 'Does that make sense to you? Do you see?'
  - Simple *Yes* answers should be treated with caution, however, so sometimes a direct request for feedback might be necessary.
  - 'This is really important, so can I just check what you've understood from what I've said?'
  - 'So, can you play it back to me?'

- Hitting the *reset button* is sometimes necessary or useful if the conversation is losing its way.

  - 'I'm sorry – I've lost my thread here.'
  - 'Why are we talking about this again?'
  - 'I'm not sure I'm making myself clear. What are you hearing?'

Channel Choice refers to picking the right communication channel for your message from the many on offer nowadays – face-to-face, phone, text, email, social media and so on. Each channel has its pros and its cons and channel choice starts with understanding what these are. The gold standard is face-to-face-same-space communication, where each person is fully aware of the other's physical presence – body language, tone of voice, facial expression – and can check their understanding in real time. Every other form of communication removes one or more element of that gold standard, so it's important to realise how this can help or hinder what you're trying to share via each particular channel.

Conversation Management

As with any new skill, consistently sticking to the *Three Attitudes* and *Three Practices* of creative conversation can be difficult. Old habits die hard and, for something we do all the time, talking can often end up creating a bit of a mess. Who hasn't lost control of a conversation by using the wrong words, blurting things out or going off on a tangent? And these are just three of many things that can cause things to go wrong.

That's where your *Conversation Manager* comes in. This is the name Osborn and Canfor-Dumas give in *The Talking Revolution* to the inner voice we all have that's constantly talking to us in one ear, while we're trying to understand with the other.

- 'I'm such a fraud - she really knows her stuff.'

- 'I just wish he would just listen to me.'
- 'I haven't got time for this.'
- 'Oops – that didn't come out right.'

These thoughts often have nothing to do with the explicit subject of the conversation but form our view of its underlying process. However, by becoming more aware of your *Conversation Manager,* you can start to consciously use that inner voice to decide who you talk to – and when, where, about what, and how – in a way that intentionally aims to create value.

How Do You Make Your Conversation Manager Work For You?

Getting to know your *Conversation Manager* can be tricky. We're not used to thinking consciously about the process of our conversations as well as their content while talking with someone. The whole thing is usually just intuitive and unconscious, which is why it's necessary to steadily *train* your *Conversation Manager* – to be able to kick in just when they're needed.

As with learning any skill, intentionally managing a conversation can feel clumsy and awkward at first, but as we explained earlier *(See p74)* there are four steps you can take to gradually integrate this skill into your daily interactions – *unconscious incompetence, conscious incompetence, conscious competence, unconscious competence.*

Once you reach this fourth stage, as *The Talking Revolution* puts it, 'Our *Conversation Manager* is fully integrated into how we think and act, always watchful but discreetly, in the background, like an attentive instructor. Even so, at crucial moments, they will spring forward to remind us of the *Three [Attitudes]* or the *Three Practices*, so that our conversation can be steered (back) in a positive, creative direction.'

How Do You Set The Right Conditions For A Creative Conversation?

Your *Conversation Manager* doesn't just oversee the ins and outs of a creative conversation when it's in progress; they also have a hand in setting the right conditions for it to start on the best possible foundation. For example, they might suggest you do a little mental pre-planning for an important conversation by asking these questions:

- Do I want primarily to understand something or be understood?
- Or do I maybe just want to open up a subject and examine it together?
- Is there something I particularly want to challenge? Or do I want to be challenged – and how will I respond if I am?
- How will I take responsibility for this conversation?
- How can I make sure I'll stay open, especially if I hear something I don't like?
- How can I create the maximum value during the conversation?

Simple preparation like this can really help a conversation get off on the right foot and stay positive, even if it hits a difficult bump.

Developing the habit of considering Kipling's *Six Honest Serving Men* – plus the honorary seventh, Whether – can also be very helpful in addressing potential problems before they arise.

- Who are we talking to?
- What are we talking about?
- When are we talking?
- Where are we talking?
- How are we talking? (aka *Channel Choice*)
- Whether to talk?

By asking these questions, your *Conversation Manager* prompts you to think about the central purpose of creative conversation, which is to try to create *something of value* in every conversation. So, as the honorary seventh *Serving-Man* suggests, sometimes it might be better not to have that conversation at all…

Exercise

Over the next week, as you start to use the Three Attitudes and Three Practices to make your communication more effective, spend a couple of minutes at the end of every conversation to take note of one thing you might have done before you started the conversation that you feel would have improved the result.

At the end of the week, take a look at what you have written down.

Can you see any patterns?

What can you do to improve things?

Summary

No-one likes conflict but avoiding it can be very destructive to your enterprise and your wellbeing.

This chapter focuses on how you can help yourself and your organisation by developing clear and effective habits of communication to turn the conflicts we run from into opportunities for creativity and positive change.

We set out how we can all develop the ability to hold *creative conversations,* which seek to create *something of value* from every verbal exchange. It explains how developing three key attitudes and three key practices can help you do this and how being aware of and then managing your inner voice is vital for success.

The foundation stones of effective communication lie in three key attitudes:

1. *Personal Responsibility* is about taking personal responsibility first for the thoughts, feelings, words, tone and actions on your side of any communication, in order to guide things in a positive direction; and second, for your own, unique communication network, understanding that as you change, so will this network.
2. *Openness* is about being open to hearing and understanding the attitudes of other people, to what they care about, even if you disagree with them.
3. *Creativity* is about focusing on creating something of value from the inevitable twists and turns of any communication.

These *Three Attitudes* need to be supported by three key practices:

1. *Understanding First* is about developing the discipline of focusing on, and achieving clarity about what the other person is saying as the starting point in any conversation.
2. *Challenging* is about testing what's being said in a way that opens things up and leads to greater clarity and connection, rather than shutting things down or causing an argument.
3. *Being Understood* is about focusing on the needs of the listener to ensure that what we ourselves *transmit* is received with clarity and understanding by them.

In each case we've offered some simple guidelines to help you put theory into practice, including on how to become more skilled at *channel choice* by recognising the potential and limitations of each communication channel.

This is all held together by your *Conversation Manager*, your inner voice that monitors and guides your conversations and also aims to set the optimum conditions for a creative conversation to take place. With practice and commitment, our Conversation Manager can become as much a part of how we talk and listen to others as road-sense becomes a part of a driver's consciousness.

The rewards are significant.

'Spend more time listening than talking.'

Alisha Fernandez Miranda, *CEO IG Consulting*

Part 6
Clarity Of Meetings

Part 6
Introduction To Clarity of Meetings

'Your meetings should be passionate, intense, exhausting – and never boring.'

Patrick Lencioni, *The Four Obsessions of an Extraordinary Executive*

Meetings don't generally get a great press, do they?

Rightly so, in many cases. But whenever you have a group of people in a room together – large or small, scheduled or unscheduled – they're more than likely trying to achieve something. And if people are an organisation's most valuable asset, exactly how we bring them together and use their time and talents in meetings has a massive bearing on the health of the whole enterprise.

A meeting can quicken your pulse or slow it right down as we all know, so it's crucial to get it right. Effective meeting management must be considered not just tactically as a tool or a process, but as a culture. This requires a clear overall approach to how you plan, run, review and improve meetings.

Some leaders, it's true, have more of an aptitude for running meetings than others – but to achieve the most productive culture, all leaders need to be able to run great meetings.

In this final part of the book we aim to show how it's possible to achieve this by incorporating all seven of our principles into three simple meeting structures and create a highly effective meeting system.

Chapter 15
Clarity of Meetings

Exercise

Let's start the chapter by getting you to consider three key internal meetings you've had in the last month. Give each one a mark out of 10 for effectiveness and list three things you feel you could have done to improve that mark by 2.

What Are The Key Issues In Achieving Effective Meetings?

In 2019 online scheduling service *Doodle* released their *2019 State of Meetings Report*. It included the results of more than 6,500 interviews with working professionals in the USA, UK and Germany, with a combined experience of 19 million meetings. Some key findings include:

- 100% described poorly organised meetings as a waste of time or money. The interviewees said that they spent an average of two hours in pointless meetings every week. *Doodle* calculated this as an avoidable annual loss of £45bn!
- An average of 72% of professionals in the UK felt they lost time every week due to unnecessary or cancelled meetings.

- 40% said that poorly organised meetings mean 'I don't have enough time to do the rest of my work.'
- 43% felt that unclear actions arising from poorly organised meetings lead to confusion.
- 38 % felt that bad organisation associated with poorly organised meetings results in a loss of focus on projects.
- 31% that irrelevant attendees at poorly organised meetings slow progress.

The interviewees also identified the key elements of a successful meeting:

- 72% said setting clear objectives
- 67% said having a clear agenda
- 35% said not having too many people in the room

The biggest irritants highlighted by interviewees were:

- 55% – taking phone calls or making texts
- 50% – people who interrupt others
- 49% – people who don't listen to others
- 49% – arriving late or leaving early
- 46% – people who talk about nothing for long periods of time

These responses are very clear. So, what can you do about it?

It starts by recognising the importance of the key role in any meeting, the person responsible for making it a success, is the Chair. In many cases this will be you but it could be anyone – as long as there is clarity about the role.

What Makes An Effective Chair?

An effective Chair focuses on three key areas consistent with the three Principles of *Clarity of Measurement, Execution and Communication*. Specifically, an effective Chair:

- *Drives accountability* by ensuring that all decisions on specific actions:
    - have a clear measurable and agreed outcome that defines success; and that
    - responsibility to achieve that outcome rests clearly with a specific individual who has attended the meeting.
- *Plans meticulously* using the tools like the *Impact Filter* and the six planning questions to make sure:
    - the purpose of the meeting is clear
    - the agenda serves that purpose
    - it's held at the best time and in the best location
    - the right people attend
    - they come with the necessary resources
    - clear measures of success are considered
    - any conflict that might arise from people being challenged, both by you and each other, is prepared for
- *Adopts a coaching mindset* and uses the key habits of *Clarity of Communication* to:
    - focus all discussions, by defining and then referencing the purpose at all times
    - maximise the value from the people in the room by understanding first.
    - ask open questions so that people feel (and are) heard
    - build on ideas as they arise, rather than cutting them off or ignoring them

- summarise concisely to confirm understanding
- manage the energy curve

To expand on this last point, the most productive meetings come from everyone being enthused and focused, so a Chair needs to make sure everyone achieves that state as quickly as possible. It's essential, though, to bring everyone back to an even keel at the end and focus on the need for clearly delegated action. This requires time and the discipline to clarify and summarise agreed actions and responsibilities, no matter how energetic things have become. This whole process is called *managing the energy curve (See Figure 16.1 below).*

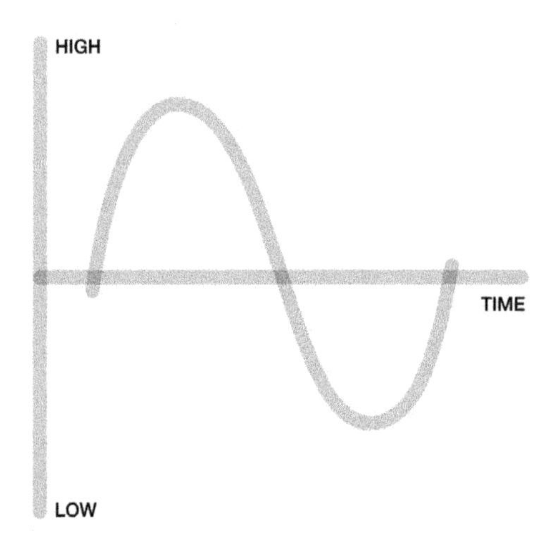

Figure 16.1 The Energy Curve Of A Meeting

What Makes An Effective Participant?

It's not just the Chair's responsibility to make an effective meeting. The other participants clearly have an essential role to play too.

Everyone attending can contribute to the meeting's success in the following ways:

- *Preparation* – Participants have the responsibility to prepare anything they need to maximise their contribution. This includes their own numbers/data and information on whatever they have agreed to take responsibility for.
- *Energy* – Everyone needs to show up with energy and enthusiasm. To be passionate and courageous about solving problems; to be prepared to challenge and have tough conversations if necessary, all the while using your values as a compass.
- *Timing* - Everyone should arrive five minutes before the start time, so they're ready to begin promptly. Arriving early enables everyone to be mindful of the need to transition from *working in* to *working on* the business.
- *Technology* - Everyone should put away their phones. If you have to use a computer during the meeting, make sure the email notifications are switched off to minimise interruptions and maximise focus.
- *Pace* – All reporting should be focused and concise, to maximise the use of time.
- *Brevity* – At all points less is more, especially when reporting to the group where which should ideally take no more than a minute for each person. Achieving this does require more thought and preparation before the meeting.

Once the Chair is clear of their overall responsibilities there are many ways to run an effective meeting, but we believe that the maximum value comes from working within three distinct formats:

- Quarterly Strategy Meetings
- Weekly Team Meetings
- Everyday meetings

Let's look at them each in turn.

Quarterly Strategy Meeting

Why Have A Quarterly Strategy Meeting?

The SOAP structure we introduced in Chapter 7 is a highly effective tool to enable you, as the leader, to delegate responsibility clearly throughout your enterprise as you map out your global strategy in a clear cascade of pages.

The purpose of the *Quarterly Strategy Meeting (QSM)* is to build your confidence in this process. It ensures you have the consistent opportunity to hold everyone accountable for their actions; specifically, for the commitments they've made to achieve specific goals in the previous 90-day period within the context of their pages. It also gives you the chance to address any significant issues that are impeding progress.

What Does A Quarterly Strategy Meeting Involve?

A *QSM* is a review of the overall strategic plan, plus the individual plans of the key members of the team. In your case, this means the plans of your Senior Leadership Team.

So a *QSM* centres on reviewing progress on the agreed goals that were set for the previous 90 days and agreeing the goals for the coming 90 days. The *QRM* should include highlighting any barriers the team members feel are limiting their progress. Time should also be allocated to consider solutions to key issues that have either not had sufficient discussion during the weekly meeting *(See p232)* or were not relevant to that structure.

Who Is Involved In The Quarterly Strategy Meeting?

The *QSM* needs to involve your Senior Leadership Team, although it's equally useful for any team leader – at any level – to drive accountability for execution within their teams.

Bear in mind, too, that while as the leader you drive the planning of the meeting, you might find it useful to employ a third-party facilitator to lead the session as this can free you up to participate, until such point that some of the key practices of measurement, accountability communication are fully embedded in your culture.

When Does The Quarterly Strategy Meeting Happen?

As its name suggests, a *QSM* is held every three months/ 90 days throughout the year. We recommend devoting a half-day (minimum) on it and a full working day for at least two of the *QSMs* each year.

Where Does The Quarterly Strategy Meeting Happen?

Ideally, the *QSM* should be held away from any distraction, where everyone in the room can give their full attention. Subject to your budget, this could include a location that's not your regular workplace.

How Is The Quarterly Strategy Meeting Structured?

To use the meeting time efficiently, we recommend that each participant spends about twenty minutes reporting on the following basis:

- Confirm current strategy
- Goals for last 90 days
- Successes
- Challenges
- Goals for next 90 days

As the leader of the organisation you start with a review of the overall strategy, plus a progress report on your key pages highlighting any barriers to success that you might facing. These barriers should be noted down as they arise but not addressed. Each member of the team then follows your lead.

Once everyone is finished, you then have time to use the collective knowledge and expertise of the team to prioritise the list using Covey's *Time Management Matrix* outlined in Chapter 3. This will reveal what is most important and/or urgent. Then look at all the barriers you have listed in turn, using the approach outlined below.

Beware, though, that while a *QSM* can allow more time for discussion than other meetings, it's easy for things to meander. So, as Chair, you need to maintain a consistent, disciplined approach to this. As with all meetings, time-management is essential, as is the need to conclude the *QSM* by confirming key actions.

A 5-Step Process For Addressing Barriers

We feel that addressing *Barriers* works best in five distinct steps.

- *Clarify the Barrier* – The person who has the issue looks to summarise it in one minute, defining the question they'd like answered in a simple sentence.
- *Discuss* – Everyone then has an opportunity to ask questions of clarification. One person speaks at a time and everyone who wants to participate should. The Chair needs to maintain the group's focus on trying to find the root cause of the *Barrier* and then summarise/clarify it for everyone.
- *Solutions* – People suggest thoughts, concerns and ideas for possible solutions. If I was you I would... Again, brevity is the aim. The Chair's job is to create an open, honest and safe environment for discussion, to ensure that no one talks too much and everyone gets a chance to contribute, and to summarise what's been offered.
- *Confirmation of what's been heard* – The person who's presented the problem summarises what they've heard as potential solutions.
- *Confirm Next Step*s – The Chair prompts the team to commit to a consensus on what they feel is the best next step. This is likely to be a simple *To do* (or series of *To do's*) rather than the definitive solution, so add it/them to the *To Do* list. Each *To Do* can only have one owner.

Weekly Team Meeting

Why Have A Weekly Team Meeting?

Having set out the strategy and agreed the 90 days goals for each team member within the *QSM*, the weekly meeting provides a way to monitor accountability, improve communication and crucially find solutions to problems before they get too big.

Almost every leader we know has a weekly meeting with their Senior Team. But it's often used for a simple exchange of information rather than as a vehicle to drive strategy. The result is that potential value is lost, as well as time and – crucially – enthusiasm. It's a major problem.

We believe that the one-page weekly meeting agenda developed by *EOS - Entrepreneur Operating System Inc* and pictured in *Fig 16.2* helps address this. It contains eight key elements:

- Date and time of the Meeting
- Good News
- Scorecard
- 90-Day goals
- People
- To Do
- Barriers
- Conclusion

Weekly Strategy Meeting

Date: ____________ Time: ____________

Good News: (5mins) Business or personal

Scorecard: (5mins) Are BGI's on or off track?

90 Day Review: (5mins) Are core objectives on or off track?

People: (5mins) Customer/employee successes or concerns

To Do: (5mins) Problems dealt with in last 7 days and to be dealt with in next 7 days

Barriers: (60mins) Clarify to understand, Discuss, Decide and put with an owner

Conclusion: (5mins) See bottom 4 actions

Who	To Do

Priority	Who	Challenges

- Have everyone confirm what they have committed to do
- Review what needs to be communicated and add to the To-Do list
- Give meeting a mark out of 10, in terms of accomplishment/quality of process: ☐
- What could have improved this mark? Put any answers on the To-Do list

Figure 16.2 Weekly Strategy Meeting

Before we explain how each element works, though, let's consider some key questions that relate to the preparations that any leader needs to ensure this format works successfully.

Who Attends The Weekly Meeting?

Weekly meetings should be held by teams, at all levels, and attended by members of those teams. But try to define your team as tightly as you can – who really needs to be there? The quality of outcomes of the meeting is very dependent on the quality of relationships in the room, especially the level of trust and understanding that exists between people.

This balance can be easily disrupted by people who are not accepted or seen to be within the group. It can also be disrupted by uneven levels of commitment, focus and contribution from different team members.

In your case, as the leader, we suggest that the weekly meeting includes just your immediate Senior Leadership Team and that any inconsistent behaviour is addressed immediately and openly. The joy of this structure, though, is that it can be applied to any level of an organisation where someone is leading a team of people.

Who Should Run The Weekly Meeting?

Running the weekly meeting is best done in partnership by those attending, as follows:

- The Chair acts as a facilitator to manage the agenda and keep everyone on track and to time. This doesn't always have to be you as the leader; it could be anyone in your team, as long as they have the skills for the job.
- An administrator updates the agenda during the meeting (noting issues and compiling the *To do* list) and the scorecard - the *Business Growth Indicators (BGIs)* agreed for that team. The administrator is also responsible for saving the finished record of the meeting to be ready to create the agenda for the next weekly meeting, as well as managing any technical support that is required e.g. projector/AV to help share the agenda.

- The rest of the team are there to report and problem solve – either for themselves or in support of others.

When Should The Weekly Meeting Take Place?

Ideally, the weekly meeting should happen on the same day and at the same time each week. Crucially, it needs to start and finish on time, so people need to arrive five minutes early to be ready and settled by the scheduled start time. This requires firm leadership by the Chair but is essential for the discipline and productivity. It must simply be unacceptable to arrive late or leave early unless this has already been agreed for a good reason.

Where Should The Weekly Meeting Take Place?

Ideally, again, the weekly meeting should be held in the same space each week; a quiet room with enough space for everyone to sit comfortably, a table to make note-taking easy, a visible clock and preferably a screen to make the agenda visible in live time.

How Should The Key Elements Of The Weekly Meeting Work?

While we've sought to look at most things in this book from a strategic level, the success of the weekly meeting is very dependent on the application of some very specific ideas. To that end we will now look at the key elements of the *Weekly Team Agenda* in detail as we've found that missing certain things out will have a significant negative impact on the overall effectiveness of the tool.

1. *Date and time of the Meeting* – Schedule the same time and day every week to create a routine.

2. *Good News (5 mins)* – The Chair goes around the table and gets people to do a quick share of a positive piece of personal or business news since the last meeting. This is intended as a warm-up to move people from a mindset of working in the business to working on the business. It helps set the energy level by starting things on a positive note and it's also an opportunity to get a sense of everyone's mood, just in case someone is feeling down.

3. *Scorecard (5 mins)* – This is where the rubber of your *Clarity of Measurement* really hits the road. The scorecard contains a list of weekly, activity-based numbers founded on your *BGIs* and agreed in the *QSM* that everyone uses to track their progress within the context of their *SOAP* pages. As every team member is responsible for a key area of the business or section of their specific team's business, at least one of their numbers should be the same as the number for that area as a whole. The card should be filled in beforehand and projected or printed so that everyone can see it and people should simply report if their numbers are ahead, behind or on schedule. Your job as Chair is to keep an eye out for trends – we suggest at least six weeks of figures that are heading in the same direction – and hold people accountable if they haven't flagged up the trend themselves. The key is not to try to address issues at this point. If a number isn't what's expected it goes straight to the *Barriers* list for consideration later in the meeting. *(For troubleshooting see p238).*

4. *90-Day goals (5 mins)* – Every person will have highlighted their 8-10 goals in the *QRM* and The Chair asks them in turn if they're on or off-track. If they're off-track, they can be asked if they feel they'd benefit from putting that goal on the *Barriers* list or would like to arrange another meeting specifically to discuss potential solutions.

5. *People (5 mins)* – This is the opportunity to share any successes or concerns related to employees or customers. Keep headlines to a single sentence. If any further action needs to be taken to resolve problems it should be added to the *Barriers* list.

6. *To Do (5 mins)* – This is the point to review the *To Do* list from the previous week to make sure that things were actually done, ticking them off as they're confirmed.

You need to hold people to account by ensuring that when they make a commitment to do something it gets done. If it hasn't been, it's put onto the *Barriers* list (see below) so more time can be allocated to consider how these can best be addressed. *To Do* is also the time to focus on what needs to be done in the next seven days. Add fresh items to the list as they arise. As a rule of thumb, 90% of *To Do* tasks should get completed each week. Less than this is a clear indication of an accountability problem, which could in turn be one of…

7. *Barriers (60 mins)* – This is the engine of the meeting. This lists the things that have been identified by someone, either in the meeting or previously, as *Barriers* to goals being achieved. This hour offers an opportunity for the team step away from working in the business to work on it, strategically. That's why it's allocated the bulk of the time. So, how does it work?

   Step 1 - Before the section begins, the Chair checks in with everyone to see if anyone wants to add any *Barriers* to the existing list of inherited ones and those added during the meeting.

   Step 2 - In less than 30 seconds, prioritise the list using Covey's *Time Management Matrix* again as explained in the *QSM.*

   Step 3 – Using the same five-step process we outlined above on page 231, then address the barrier voted No 1. In some meetings you will solve only one issue and in others you could cover many more. The key is to make sure you're working on them in order of their priority to the overall purpose and that someone has responsibility for what needs to be done next. Then put it on the *To Do* list with the owner(s) initials and move onto the next *Barrier.*

8. *Conclusion (5 mins)* - This draws the meeting to a close, bringing the energy level down to drive action using the energy curve model we covered earlier (see page 226). Identify the next steps and collect feedback for improving the next meeting. Review all the actions and make sure each one has an owner. Consider whether anything that has arisen in the meeting needs to be shared with other people in the organisation and add that action to the *To Do* list to ensure it's done.

Finally, get everyone to rate the meeting on a scale of 1-10, where 10 means they got what they wanted from the meeting and the process worked. Get everyone to include one action that would increase their mark by 1. The suggested improvements go onto the *To Do* list.

After the meeting –The Administrator updates the agenda for the next meeting by removing the solved issues and completed *To Dos.* This should be saved in a place where everyone can access it for reference.

Top Tips For Troubleshooting Your Scorecard

- Don't overcomplicate it – there are a handful of key measures for each area of activity e.g. sales = revenue, prices, profit margin, customer satisfaction etc.
- Align the figures with your *Purpose, Vision and Values* – e.g if one of your values is collaboration you need to ensure there is a measure to consider that reflects this.
- Relate the figures to the core processes of doing business – *talent, marketing, sales, finance, social impact, operations* and *digital.*
- Ask *How do you know if you've had a good week?*

Everyday Meetings

Obviously, meetings take place all the time in your enterprise where the strategic quarterly and weekly approach are not applicable. Even so, your culture will still benefit from having a consistent approach to these everyday meetings.

The format we propose has been developed by Richard Jacobs, CEO of *The Yes Consultancy.* It offers a simple, accessible template *(See Fig 16.3)* to improve the productivity of every single meeting, whatever the status of those attending.

Everyday Meeting

Date: ______________ Time: ______________

The Purpose of the Meeting is:
What is the meeting designed to achieve? (10 words or less.) Who needs to be there to serve the Purpose?

Set Key Questions for the Meeting:

- Turn all agenda points into open questions
- Ensure they get to the heart of the matter and generate discussion
- No more than 5 questions
- Set a time limit for each question

	Time Limit	Question	Actions Specific & Measurable	Completed Time & Date
1				
2				
3				
4				
5				

Who needs to be informed and by when?

How and when will we check progress?

Figure 16.3: Everyday Meeting

It suggests that to maximise its effectiveness the Chair of the meeting considers a few basic guidelines:

1. *Coaching Mindset* – Approach the job of Chair as an enabler rather than a dictator. This comes from a belief that the meeting's purpose will be best served by valuing the contribution of everyone who attends (see point 3).
2. *Clear Purpose* – Ask yourself what you want the meeting to achieve, then write it on the agenda in twelve words or less.
3. *Attendees* - Who needs to attend to service this purpose? Consider this before you invite people. Sometimes, if you're in doubt, you can just extend the invitation widely with its purpose and agenda made clear and the recipients will decide whether to attend or not.
4. *Length of meeting* - Ideally no everyday meeting should last more than 60 minutes, which therefore limits the agenda.
5. *Agenda as Questions* - Turn all agenda items into open questions that can't be answered with a simple Yes or No. This will encourage a more effective interaction with the attendees and support your coaching mindset.
6. *Timing* - Introduce a time limit for each question/agenda item in advance. This will help you pace the meeting and make sure you cover everything.
7. *Actions* – The answers to each question/agenda item should be specific and measurable actions to be completed by a specific time and date, as this focuses everyone. There should also be agreement on who, not at the meeting, would benefit from being informed and by when; and also how progress will be monitored and measured.
8. *Summarising* – All actions points at the end of the meeting should be clearly summarised, saved and distributed to all participants, plus anyone else identified who would benefit.

Summary

In this chapter we've considered the importance of having a clear strategy for running effective meetings in any organisation. We started by considering some top tips for anyone chairing any meeting effectively and then looked at a meeting system made of up three distinct meeting structures:

1. *Quarterly Strategy Meetings* that provide the opportunity to review and adjust the annual strategy on a consistent basis.
2. *Weekly Team Meetings* that drive accountability, ensure things actually get done rather than just discussed, and that offer an opportunity to address, quickly and efficiently, the small barriers that so often get in the way of completing tasks.
3. *Everyday Meetings* that produce greater productivity by encouraging consistency in how people behave when they come together as group, no matter how small.

Each approach includes elements from each of the seven principles presented earlier in this book but particularly the three we discussed in Part 5 – *Clarity of Measurement, Execution and Communication* – that provide the day-to-day, nuts-and-bolts implementation of a clear culture.

The suggestions aren't complicated but they do work.

All you need to do now is to give them a try!

Exercise

Commit to applying the weekly and general meeting structures set out in this chapter to specific meetings you're running in the next week.

At the end of each meeting ask everyone who has attended to give it a mark out of 10 for productiveness and enjoyment; and also ask them to list three things that contributed to that mark.

Chapter 16
Next Steps

We started this book by arguing that a key part of finding solutions to many of society's challenges involves harnessing the spirit and energy of entrepreneurship within the social space. We advocated recognising this as a vital *4th Sector* of the economy that brings something very different to the mix than the other three – private, public and not-for-profit solutions such as charitable and voluntary organisations.

We explained why we feel that 4th Sector entrepreneurs are unique, driven by their enjoyment of making profit to address their passion for social impact; but also why it's important that we all recognise that the challenge of serving two masters – financial self-sufficiency and social impact – can put severe pressure on their well-being. It can be lonely and difficult being an entrepreneur – but it's even lonelier and more difficult being an entrepreneur in the *4th Sector.*

There are ways to make things easier, however, while still growing impact in a sustainable way.

It starts by making a commitment to extricate yourself from working in your enterprise to working on it. This takes courage, as it can be difficult to have the time – and the confidence in your own capability – to make that investment. But we suggest some approaches that can help manage the stress of doing this in a way that will increase overall productivity.

Having laid this foundation, we then proposed seven Principles for any leader to follow, nested in three key outcomes:

- Clarity of Leadership
- Clarity of Strategy
- Clarity of Culture

Clarity of Leadership starts with our First Principle – *Clarity of Personal Purpose and Values.* We often find leaders who suffer from confusion about what they actually want to achieve and frustration at the way people behave around them.

By being clear – not only about the impact you're really passionate about making but also what lifestyle you want, how much money that requires and the career stages you need to go through to achieve this – you can choose the best enterprise to fit your goals.

Our Second Principle focuses on how to clarify which enterprise that might be. What *Purpose* does it serve, what *Values* does it embody and what *Vision* of the future does it present? All three must be clear and congruent with your personal aims as a leader; if they're not, the friction will just make you unhappy.

Without our Third Principle, however, such congruence simply isn't sustainable. This focuses on clarifying what makes your offer unique and of value to which customer and what evidence there is that they will pay for it.

Once all is clear in leadership, the next stage involves *Clarity of Strategy,* the overall plans to achieve your results. These cover the key areas of any business – *Marketing, Sales, Finance, Operations, Digital* and *Talent* – but also one specific to the *4th Sector, Social Impact.* While we touch on how to develop these, our Fourth principle emphasises that of all strategies, *Talent* is by far and away the most important.

Our Fifth, Sixth and Seven principles form the foundation for *Clarity of Culture.*

Here we looked at the need to have a culture that is driven by measurement, that approaches every project with a consistent method of execution and that encourages everybody to develop consistent and effective habits of communication. These all run through three meeting frameworks that ensure that whenever people come to work together they have a clear structure to maximise productivity.

While we've suggested it's ideal to consider things in a specific order, like every entrepreneur you will have an instinct of what will work best for you. We're passionate about growing the *4th Sector*, so our challenge to you is to commit to the Principle that you feel will help you most in fulfilling your passion for social justice.

We know it can be scary but it will be worth it.

As the Chinese philosopher Lao Tzu said, 'A journey of a thousand miles begins with a single step.'

Start now.

We'd love to hear how you get on so please send any feedback or success stories to us at *feedback@4thsector.org.uk*

Appendices

Appendix 1: Measuring Social Value

Measuring social value/impact can be difficult and confusing. Organisations can tie themselves into knots with lots of statistical gymnastics to produce figures that are of little practical benefit.

Here we present a couple of approaches – with links to websites where you can find out more – which we suggest can be of value, not only in clarifying the social value you are looking to create, but also in clarifying some of the practical steps to take to do so practically.

Social Impact – Theory Of Change

Why Is A Theory Of Change Useful?

Judging the true social impact of a social enterprise is often vague, compromised and lost in pressures of the day-to-day operation. A *Theory of Change (TOC)* provides some clarity on the social impact you're trying to achieve, which in turn drives clarity on how its level can be measured and ultimately grown.

What Is A Theory Of Change?

A *TOC* maps out what change you believe will be achieved by what you do as an organisation. It sets out how an action (or series of actions) aims to foster change to produce some intended outcomes and impacts and the actual difference your intervention will make and how. It's not a guarantee, just a starting-point, a cause-and-effect theory, from which you can work.

Who Needs To Be Involved With Creating It?

Your *TOC* starts with your customers, the people you're looking to affect. Only they can tell you if what you're doing – or planning to do - really does/will have a positive impact.

Once you feel you have a proper understanding of their perspective, your role as the leader is to ensure that you get the input of the Board, Senior Leadership Team, your staff and as wide a range of your other stakeholders as possible. The more relevant people you can involve, the wider the understanding of the issues and the clearer your *TOC* will be, and the better the measuring data that will be collected.

When Do You Develop Your Theory Of Change?

You develop your *TOC* soon as you can to ensure that it will be built into the DNA of your organisation.

How Do You Develop It?

You start with a clear picture of the ultimate social impact you want to achieve, then test that picture with a good cross-section of your customer base – is this the impact they are looking for, too?

You then list the key specific outcomes you believe you're going to achieve.

Start with the intended outcomes for the whole organisation, but then consider the outcomes for each of your activities so you build up a coherent picture at each level.

In this way you can highlight how each level connects with the next – or doesn't.

For example, an organisation looking to support people into employment may have some intermediary outcomes – such as improved confidence and motivation – that have to happen before the individual finds employment. If you're doing things that only build confidence but don't increase motivation, your *TOC* highlights the need for a design improvement.

Beware not to confuse outcomes with outputs. Outputs are the products, services and activities that you deliver, while outcomes are the actual impacts these have on your customers/end-users – which you hope are the ones you want, of course.

Once you have identified the intended outcomes within your *TOC*, the next stage is to identify what data you need to collect to show how you're doing, positively and negatively. A consistent process of data collection should then be built into your day-to-day operations, as with the collection of financial data. By reviewing this data regularly, you'll be able to monitor your progress and adjust accordingly, seeking to improve outcomes as part of a regular cycle of continuous learning.

In other words, no *Theory of Change* is static.

For further information on *impact measurement* we recommend visiting the following two sites

http://www.inspiringimpact.org/

http://www.trustimpact.co.uk/

B Corp

Why Do We Think B Corp Certification Is Of Interest?

B Corp Certification offers a benchmark of what many consider to be best practice for running an organisation that aspires to maximise its social impact. It has its critics but we do believe that it provides a very useful to any *4th Sector* toolbox.

To that end *Bubble Chamber* followed the process to achieve *B Corp Certification* as we felt it provides a practical, transparent and independently-verifiable companion tool for you to evaluate and monitor your *Theory of Change*.

What Is B Corp Certification?

B Corp Certification seeks to embed a *mission lock* – the idea of purpose and values – into an organisation, regardless of who owns it. It combines a legal requirement to consider the benefit to all stakeholders equally, along with an assessment of how the organisation's behaviour impacts its workers, community, environment and customers.

The *B Corp* process was developed in 2006 when three friends left careers in business and private equity to create an organisation dedicated to making it easier for mission-driven companies to protect and improve their positive impact over time.

Who Decides What Is Assessed?

The standards for *B Corp Certification* are overseen by an independent committee – *B Lab's independent Standards Advisory Council* – made up of people with industry and stakeholder expertise. Its role is to oversee the content and weightings of the *B Impact Rating System*, which includes:

- Approving changes made to the *B Impact Assessment* as part of its three-year update process.

- Determining eligibility for *B Corp Certification* in cases where companies make material disclosures on the *Disclosure Questionnaire.*
- Reviewing material complaints against *Certified B Corporations.*
- Approving addenda to the *B Impact Assessmen*t created by specialised *Advisory and Working Groups.*

Who Can Qualify To Be A B Corp?

1. You have to earn the majority of your revenue from trading as a for-profit organisation and have operated for more than one year.
2. Your *Articles of Associatio*n must state that the Directors of the organisation are legally obliged to consider the impact of all their decisions on all their stakeholders (including shareholders, employees, suppliers, society and the environment). This is intended to help companies protect their mission through raising capital and leadership changes and gives entrepreneurs and directors the legal backup to factor in social impact criteria properly when evaluating potential sale and liquidity options.

How Do You Achieve B Corp Certification?

Once you confirm you qualify legally for *B Corp Certification* you need to complete a *Business Impact Assessment (BIA).*

See *bimpactassessment.net*

This is a free online platform, used by over 50,000 businesses, which evaluates how your company interacts with your workers, customers, community and the environment.

Many of the businesses that use the platform won't ever qualify as a *B Corp,* but completing the *BIA* offers a guide to how you can work towards becoming a more socially responsible company.

The *BIA* has two sets of questions on:

1. **Operations,** which covers a company's day-to-day activities
2. **Impact Business Models,** which awards additional points for business models designed specifically to create additional positive impact.

Once you've completed the *BIA* and have scored more than 80 out of the 200 points available, your responses are verified by B Lab and you'll have twelve months to make any necessary changes to meet the legal requirements for certification.

The *BIA* is updated every three years to incorporate feedback and improve upon the standards.

However, there is a certain scepticism about the *B Corp* process.

- It's possible to game it. True – just as you can massaging the figures in your audited account. The reality, though, is that the process is not as easy as it might appear and, anyway, why take the risk of cheating when it leaves you open to discovery and criticism?
- It has no legal enforcement rights. That is also true, so if someone is determined to stop being a *B Corp* they can. This does, however, require a very public statement of intent that won't be missed by any stakeholder.
- The questions measure the wrong things when it comes to impact. No questionnaire is perfect and *B Lab* are constantly improving their process.

Find out more at *https://bcorporation.net/*

Social Enterprise Mark

What Is The Social Enterprise Mark?

The only internationally available accreditation that provides external verification of your social enterprise credentials.

Why Do We Think Social Enterprise Mark Is Valuable?

It provides impartial independent proof that your organisation is creating specific social impact. It was the original social enterprise accreditation and remains the only one to externally assess the credentials of all applicants, as well as regularly reviewing the continuing eligibility of all Mark holders.

It goes further than the B Corp certification, by showing that your organisation operates primarily to make a positive difference to society and/or the environment. It offers instant credibility for all stakeholders that you are operating in the interest of wider society, and not to line shareholders' pockets.

Who Decides Who Qualifies?

All applications are assessed against a clear set of criteria (set out in the next section). The assessment process is overseen by an independent Certification Panel, which is made up of volunteers who represent expertise in business, law and social enterprise.

How Do You Qualify?

You need to be an independent business primary dedicated to social and/or environmental objectives, which earns at least 50% of income from trading and is committed to investing at least 51% of any profit towards these objectives. You must be able to demonstrate how you are striving to achieve your objectives and must also have an asset lock, where any residual assets are distributed to benefit your aims should the company be dissolved.

Find out more at *www.socialenterprisemark.org.uk*

Appendix 2: How Not To Challenge Bingo

How Not to Challenge Bingo

To have a bit of fun take this bingo card and see how many of these unproductive challenges you can spot people making in the next week.

Rejection: 'You're just wrong.'	**Condemnation/Labelling:** 'That is just racist/evil/ dishonest.'	**Devaluing the message:** 'That's completely irrelevant/ ridiculous.'
Devaluing the messenger: 'That's the sort of argument I'd expect from a six-year-old.'	**Attacking the messenger:** 'You're just too sensitive/ unfeeling.'	**Getting emotional:** 'One more word from you and I'll get so angry...'
Setting traps: 'So what you're saying is [a]? 'Yes...' 'Which means [b] – right?' 'Erm...' 'So therefore [c] – hmm?' (aka 'Gotcha!')	**Fact-bombing:** 'OK, I've heard what you think but [a fact], [b fact], [c fact], ...'	**Appealing to the crowd:** 'Well, you're in a minority of one if you think that!'
Appealing to the past: 'Why should I listen to you when you were wrong about that other thing?'	**Turning up the volume:** 'No, no, no [raises voice] No, YOU listen to ME...	**Misinterpreting:** 'So, basically, what you're saying is [a].' 'No.' Proceeds to criticise [a]

End Notes

1. Michael Porter & Mark R Kramer- 2011Creating Shared Value – Michael E Harvard Business Review, 2011 http://hbr.org/2011/01/the-big-idea-creating-shared-value
2. David Cameron - https://www.telegraph.co.uk/comment/8337239/How-we-will-release-the-grip-of-state-control.html
3. Larry Fink - https://www.blackrock.com/hk/en/insights/larry-fink-ceo-letter
4. Andy Haldane - https://www.bankofengland.co.uk/-/media/boe/files/speech/2016/the-great-divide.pdf?la=en&hash=D44B-91D2A6F39A4333ED3B92CB6870DD45E40306 September 2017.
5. Spectator - https://www.spectator.co.uk/2017/09/even-the-tories-should-admit-that-its-time-to-renationalise-the-water-companies/
6. Professor Gill Kirton & Dr Cécile Guillaume - Work, Employment and Society, British Sociological Association 2019
7. Financial Times – Helen Warrell https://www.ft.com/content/32d66096-35e9-11e9-bd3a-8b2a211d90d5 Feb 22nd 2019
8. John McDonnell - Labour Party Annual Conference 2017
9. Mariana Mazucattu – The Value of Everything Penguin 2017; William H Janeway - Doing Capitalism in the Innovation Economy: Cambridge University Press 2018
10. BIT & Gov.uk
    https://www.theguardian.com/politics/2018/nov/10/nudge-unit-pushed-way-private-sector-behavioural-insights-team

    https://www.dezeen.com/2013/04/16/gov-uk-government-website-wins-designs-of-the-year-2013/

11. Financial Times – Martin Wolf - https://www.ft.com/content/0470ad62-f623-11e7-88f7-5465a6ce1a00 January 11th 2018

12. Computerworld - https://www.computerworld.com/article/3412308/the-uk-s-worst-public-sector-it-disasters.html 15 June 2018

13. https://www.parliament.uk/business/committees/committees-a-z/commons-select/public-accounts-committee/news-parliament-2017/disclosure-barring-service-report-published-17-19/

14. https://www.socialenterprise.org.uk/What-is-it-all-about/

15. Social Enterprise Mark - https://www.socialenterprisemark.org.uk/frequently-asked-questions/ - toggle-id-1

16. B Corp - https://bcorporation.net/

17. Hidden Revolution - https://www.socialenterprise.org.uk/policy-and-research-reports/the-hidden-revolution/

18. Hidden Revolution - https://www.socialenterprise.org.uk/policy-and-research-reports/the-hidden-revolution/

19. Hidden Revolution - https://www.socialenterprise.org.uk/policy-and-research-reports/the-hidden-revolution/

20. SEUK Future of Business – State of Social Enterprise 2017

21. Kibler, Wincent, Kautonen, Cacciotti and Obschonka – Can prosocial motivation harm entrepreneurs' subjective well-being? https://www.sciencedirect.com/science/article/pii/S0883902617305669?via=ihub

22. www.alistairlobo.com

23. Stephen Covey - The 7 Habits of Highly Effective People (1989).

24. Elizabeth Dougherty- MCGovern Institute for Brain Research - news.mit.edu/2015/neurons-drive-habit=0819

25. Martin Broadwell Teaching For Learning, Feb 1969

26. Tony Robbins https://www.habitsforwellbeing.com/6-core-human-needs-by-anthony-robbins/

27. www.bgistrategy.com

28. www.eosworldwide.com

29. Peter Drucker - American management consultant, educator, and author, whose writings contributed to the philosophical and practical foundations of the modern business corporation.

30. Gallup Q12 Survey - https://q12.gallup.com/public/en-us/Features.

31. Harvard Business Review (see www.hbr.org)

32. CIPD - Resourcing and talent planning (2015), www.cipd.co.uk/knowldge/strategy/resourcing/surveys

33. The cost of the brain drain (2014)– www.oxfordeconomics.com

34. REC www.rec.uk.com www.indeed.co.uk June 2017

35. See Royal Statistical Society – www.rss.org. We also strongly recommend The Art of Statistics by David Spiegelhalter.

36. The Hammock Test courtesy of Deri Lewellyn-Davis.

37. Coined by Helmuth von Moltke the Elder, Prussian field marshall (1800-91).

38. See, for example, the famous Harvard Study (https://www.adultdevelopmentstudy.org) and the 2016 study led by Richard Layard, Emeritus Professor of Economics at the LSE, 'The Origins of Happiness' (http://assets.press.princeton.edu/chapters/i11179.pdf).

About Ben Freedman and Craig Carey

Ben Freedman and Craig Carey set up *Bubble Chamber CIC* in 2014. Contact them at: *www.bubblechamber.net* or *LinkedIn.*

The purpose of *Bubble Chamber* is to help leaders of *4th Sector* Enterprises gain the clarity and courage they need to grow their social impact.

Ben helped found two national charities, *Aspire,* the UK's leading *Spinal Injuries Charity* and *Breakthrough Breast Cancer,* now the UK's largest *Breast Cancer Charity* and was a founding participant member of *Pilotlight.* He is also the owner of the *Prince Charles Cinema* in Central London as well as *Singalonga Productions* that produces film and theatre events worldwide.

Craig has 20 plus years' experience working as a business coach, consultant, non-exec and advisor across a range of different sectors – charity, social enterprise, NGO, SME and finance (specialising in insolvency and business turnaround).

Craig has previously worked at *Social Enterprise UK* and *Pilotlight*. Craig has an MBA and a degree in Economics and is an accredited practitioner for *Strategy on a Page, Harrison Assessments* and *Talent Dynamics.*

https://www.linkedin.com/in/craig-carey-5103b11a/

Lightning Source UK Ltd.
Milton Keynes UK
UKHW020621040220
358132UK00012B/780